John 316

Kids DVD

Kerasal

You can
F your PREDICT
UTURE

You can
*Y*ou *can*
your PREDICT
FUTURE

Tom
BROWN

Whitaker House

YOU CAN PREDICT YOUR FUTURE

Pastor Tom Brown
P. O. Box 27275
El Paso, TX 79926

ISBN: 0-88368-386-5
Printed in the United States of America
Copyright © 1996 by Tom Brown

Whitaker House
580 Pittsburgh Street
Springdale, PA 15144

Contents

Foreword

Several years ago, I had a listening experience which ministered greatly to my life. It was Pastor Tom Brown's audio-cassette series, *You Can Predict Your Future*. It challenged me about what to say and what not to say in receiving God's best for my life. Now Tom has produced this life-changing message in printed form. I personally predict that this message will be used by God to change many lives for the better.

The principles which Tom Brown presents in this book are clearly based on God's Word. They are sound—and so very practical. These truths have burned in Pastor Tom's heart for several years. He has written with clarity and by the rich anointing of the Holy Spirit.

You have this book in your hands. As you read, allow the Holy Spirit to guide you into these Bible principles which are destined to minister greatly to your life. God has a wonderful plan and purpose for your life. Tom

Brown's book will enhance your moving into God's best as you open your heart to the powerful truths that he mentions.

The love and fellowship of Tom and his wife, Sonia Brown, have meant much to me. Tom and Sonia realize that we will have all of eternity to tell of the victories won for Christ—but we have only a few hours before "sunset" to win them. I thank God for the holy angels who faithfully attend Tom and Sonia's ministry of excellence. They have heard the high call: "Who will go for us?" and we have answered, "Here am I. Send me" (Isa. 6:8).

> *Let not the wise man boast of his wisdom or the strong man boast of his strength or the rich man boast of his riches, but let him who boasts boast about this: that he understands and knows me, that I am the LORD, who exercises kindness, justice and righteousness on earth, for in these I delight.*   *(Jer. 9:23–24)*

I believe that God delights in Tom and Sonia Brown!

Dr. Don E. Gossett
Blaine, Washington

Introduction

The past is over and the future has started. You'll never have a chance to live the past again. For some, that's a relief.

God is a God of new beginnings. The Bible has a lot to say about new things: a new covenant, a new creation, a new Jerusalem, a new heaven, and a new earth. God is into new things.

You're about to enter a new time that no one has ever entered before—the future. What will your future hold for you? Will it be filled with happiness, achievement, health, and prosperity?

If you answer, "Well, I hope so," then go to your calendar and write on this date: Today was the beginning of my failure, because I hoped for a good future, instead of believing for a good future. Hope is good. But hope alone cannot guarantee a good future. Only faith can guarantee a good future. This book is about that kind of faith.

This is not a book about my theory. It is a book about reality—more than reality, ultimate reality. It is about God's reality. His reality is found in His Word, the Bible.

You will learn how to take God's Word, believe it correctly, and confess it out of your mouth properly in order to predict your future. Before you put this book down and say, "I've already heard the message on faith and positive confession," please continue reading. This book begins where present faith-teaching ends. It answers questions that few, if any, faith books have answered.

For example, we all know of times when our words have failed to come to pass. Most of the time we were eventually glad that they did not come to pass. I'm sure King David was glad that his negative words, "I shall perish someday by the hand of Saul" (1 Sam. 27:1), did not come to pass.

A mother and father may stay up late at night, worrying over their son who is late coming home. The woman speaks of her fears, "I just know our son has gotten into an accident. He's probably in the hospital. Let's call the hospital to see if he's there."

The husband says, "I think you're right. Let's call now."

As they are dialing the nearest hospital, their son walks in safe and sound. I'm sure the parents are relieved that their words did not come to pass.

How would you like to receive everything you say? Before you answer, think about it. Is everything which comes out of your mouth good? If not, then you ought to thank God that you don't receive everything you say.

The times that we get upset when our words fail to come to pass are when we speak God's Word, such as "My God shall supply all my needs," "I resist the devil and he flees from me," or "I am healed by the stripes of Jesus and no disease can touch my body." When those words don't come to pass, then we get mad.

"I don't understand why I'm not getting what I'm saying," you yell. "I'm speaking the Word of God, so I don't understand why my words are not coming to pass like the Bible says they should."

Since some people fail to receive what they confess, many assume that the confession of God's Word does not work. Listen, the confession of God's Word does work! However, the power of confession cannot be treated as a lucky charm or a magic wand, where you use it when you have a need. The confession of God's Word must be a way of life.

This book is going to explain why confession works, why sometimes confession doesn't work, and most importantly, how you can make confession work better for you.

Let me warn you: you will not be able to read this book fast. There are some things in this book which you might be unsure about, but don't let those things stop you from receiving all that God has for you. You will find answers to many of the questions that you've been wanting answered for years. You'll have to pause at times in order to digest the revelations in it, but it will be worth it.

You're about to embark on a journey, to the realm of faith where everything becomes possible. The message in this book has already changed the lives of millions. It has changed my life, and I know it will change your life too.

Chapter 1

Revelation, Meditation, and Proclamation

A few years back, I was at a local restaurant drinking some delicious coffee and enjoying my Bible. I was reading through the Psalms when chapter thirty-nine struck me. The wonderful smell of the coffee vanished. The people at the restaurant seemed to fade. All I could see and hear was,

> *My heart grew hot within me, and as I meditated, the fire burned; then I spoke with my tongue.* (Ps. 39:3)

When I read those profound, yet simple words, God spoke to me. He spoke only three words: "Revelation, meditation, and proclamation." I saw it! It was as though a beam of light entered my heart. I understood what God was saying to me. He was saying that first comes revelation, second comes meditation. When you have experienced revelation and practiced meditation, then you are ready to make your proclamation.

You see, many people fail in their confession because they don't have any personal revelation of the things they are confessing. They say that they are healed, prosperous, and blessed, but they don't have a revelation of these blessings, nor do they meditate on them. As a result, their confessions don't work.

Heartburn

David said, "Then I spoke" (Ps. 39:3). **"Then"** means next in order of time. Before he spoke with his tongue, David went through two phases. First he said, "My heart grew hot within me." Second he said, "And as I meditated, the fire burned." Notice these two stages: His heart grew hot, and he meditated.

What did David mean when he said that his heart grew hot? Well, he was not talking about heartburn. He did not need Rolaids.

The heart is the spirit of man. The spirit of man is the real you made in God's image. It is the place of real spiritual power. The heart is where you believe. By believing with the heart, you are saved.

David used the word "heart" to speak of his spirit, and he used the word "fire" to describe a spiritual experience. He was saying that spiritual insight came to him. The New Testament uses the word "revelation." Revelation is supernatural insight into the mind of God.

David was saying, "I have received supernatural insight into the mind of God. I know what God is thinking at this moment. I know what's on His mind. I know His perfect will."

Do you see what I'm saying? Before your confession of God's Word can work for you, you must receive revelation. This is what Paul prayed for in Ephesians 1:17: "I keep asking that the God of our Lord Jesus Christ, the glorious Father, may give you the Spirit of wisdom and revelation." There it is—the Spirit of revelation.

He goes on to pray,

> *I pray also that the eyes of your heart may be enlightened in order that you may know the hope to which he has called you, the riches of his glorious inheritance in the saints, and his incomparably great power for us who believe.*
> *(Eph. 1:18–19)*

He prayed that the eyes of their hearts would be **enlightened**. The word *enlighten* comes from two words: *en* which means "in" and *light* which means "fire." To be enlightened is to have a fire within you. The heart is enlightened by fire, and the fire is the Holy Spirit. "Do not put out the Spirit's fire" (1 Thess. 5:19).

Paul prayed that the Holy Spirit would open their spiritual understanding so that they could know three things: first, the hope of their calling; second, the inheritance within them; and third, the power that is available for them.

This is the most important prayer to pray, because the greatest need in the body of Christ is revelation. Once the church receives revelation, nothing can stop it.

Since the Holy Spirit is the person who gives us revelation, it is vital, therefore, that every Christian receive the Holy Spirit. Many Christians have unfortunately been taught that they automatically receive the Spirit at conversion, but this is simply not true. The Holy Spirit can only be received after a person is saved (John 14:17; Acts 19:1–7).

Road to Emmaus

Many people pray for revelation but don't receive it because they have too many burdens on their hearts. There is a fascinating story in the Bible which illustrates the need to cast your cares on the Lord in order to receive revelation. The story involves the resurrected Christ and two disciples who were traveling on the road to Emmaus.

> *Now the same day two of them were going to a village called Emmaus, about seven miles from Jerusalem. They were talking with each other about everything that had happened. As they talked and discussed these things with each other, Jesus himself came up and walked along with them; but they were kept from recognizing him.*   *(Luke 24:13–16)*

My question is simple. Why were they kept from recognizing Jesus? The answer is in verse seventeen: "They stood still, their faces downcast."

Do you see what their problem was? They were depressed. They had a lot on their hearts—things that had weighed them down. So Jesus, instead of telling them that He was Jesus, asked them many questions in order for them to get their burdens off their chests.

Doesn't it feel good to talk with someone about your burdens, especially when it is the

Lord? When you do, you feel a hundred pounds lighter.

You see, a bad time to study the Bible is when you are depressed. You will not get anything from your study. Revelation will not come when you are depressed. It is important to cast your cares on the Lord before you study the Bible. When you do, you are better prepared to study the Bible because you are free to receive revelation from it.

After the two disciples had shared their burdens, Jesus started to talk with them about the Scriptures. Jesus began to explain to them from the Scriptures that the Messiah had to first suffer before He could enter His glory.

> *He [Jesus] said to them, "How foolish you are, and how slow of heart to believe all that the prophets have spoken! Did not the Christ have to suffer these things and then enter his glory? And beginning with Moses and all the Prophets, he explained to them what was said in all the Scriptures concerning himself. As they approached the village to which they were going, Jesus acted as if he were going farther. But they urged him strongly, "Stay with us, for it is nearly*

evening; the day is almost over." So he
went in to stay with them.
(Luke 24:25–29)

We learn that depression is caused by being slow to believe the Bible. We also discover
that revelation does **not** come quickly when a
person is depressed.

You see, Jesus tested them. He pretended
to go farther. He wanted to see if they were
going to diligently study the Scriptures or if
they were content with their Bible study on
the road. Thankfully, these disciples wanted
more. They made Christ teach them the Bible
at their home.

We must be like them. A little Bible study
will not do. We must dig deep in the Word of
God in order to get revelation.

Then their eyes were opened and they
recognized him, and he disappeared
from their sight. They asked each other,
"Were not our hearts burning within us
while he talked with us on the road and
opened the Scriptures to us?"
(Luke 24:31–32)

I find it interesting that the thing which
the disciples found wonderful was the fact that

their **hearts burned within them** as they learned the Word of God. Notice that they did not talk about Jesus disappearing. They were more excited about their hearts burning than about Jesus supernaturally disappearing. Revelation is by far the greatest spiritual experience that anyone can receive, even greater than seeing Christ in the flesh.

So the two main lessons we learn from this story are: to cast our burdens and cares on the Lord, and then, to diligently study the Scriptures until we receive revelation knowledge.

Meditate

Once your heart grows hot, you must meditate on the revelation that you received in order to start the fire. It's not good enough to simply have a warm heart; you need a fire.

Many people are content to receive revelation, but they stop there. They don't go further by meditating on the Word of God. You must continue to meditate on your revelation. Don't stop simply with the revelation; continue until the heat turns into a fire. Only then are you going to have the spiritual force to make your words come to pass.

"Meditate" means to think deeply about something until subconsciously you begin to speak it to yourself. The Hebrew word for meditation means to mutter. "Mutter" means that you speak to yourself in a low tone of voice.

Have you ever thought so deeply about something that you unconsciously started to move your lips? Perhaps you thought about asking your boss for a raise. So on your way to work, you went over in your mind what you were going to say, and as you did, you detected that someone was staring at you. And as your eyes look up to see who it was, you blushed because you had been talking to yourself. Do you know what you were doing? You were meditating.

So to meditate means to be so absorbed with certain thoughts that we talk to ourselves. We should be so absorbed with the Word of God that we talk it to ourselves without realizing it.

Meditation has been one of the most beneficial things in my life. It has also made people wonder if I was crazy. When I used to work for a pizza parlor, I would constantly meditate on the Word of God. Often, my fellow employees would interrupt me, "Hey, Tom, what are you babbling about?"

I would blush, "I...I...I...was just thinking about the Bible." Oh, I was embarrassed, but the growth in my life was incredible. I would rather have people think that I'm crazy than fail to meditate. Anyway, many of my fellow workers are now members of my church, and they are doing what I did.

Chew the Cud

In the Old Testament, God gave Israel permission to eat any animal that chewed the cud. A cow is an example. A cow takes its time to chew. Slowly it crushes the hay and masticates the food. After minutes of gnawing down the hay into small particles, it swallows. Gulp! The first of three stomachs breaks down the food into vitamins and minerals. Soon, the cow regurgitates the food and starts the process of chewing it again. And after some time, it swallows the food once more.

The food then passes into his second stomach where it undergoes another process of digestion. After hours, the food is passed into the third stomach, where every remaining vitamin that can be drawn out is absorbed. The rest is discharged. The whole process takes about twenty-four hours.

Now, I've brought all this up to show the process of meditation. We should be like the cow and slowly chew the Word of God before we swallow. We can meditate by taking a few Scriptures and mulling them over in our minds. After we have done that a few times, we bring back those Scriptures again and start the process once more. We keep that up until the Word becomes a part of us.

Unfortunately, most people feed on the Word like a pig feeds on slop. The pig, unlike the cow, was considered an unclean animal. A pig swallows the food without hardly chewing it. In just a matter of six hours, the food is part of the pig's body. Very little nutrition from the food is absorbed by the pig, because he eats his food in a hurry. This is the way most people read their Bibles—in a hurry. This explains why most do not get much out of the Bible.

People often wonder how to study the Bible. There are many good ways, but the best way is to meditate on those portions of the Scriptures that God has used to warm your heart. Study those parts that your heart has received revelation from.

When you start to meditate, the heart that was warm will catch on fire. When it does, you are ready to make your proclamation. Your confession will at that time have power and come to pass. Your words will become more powerful, and they will work to predict your future.

You Can Predict Your Future
by saying...

My heart grows hot within me, and as I meditate, the fire burns; then I speak with my tongue.

My tongue is the pen of a skillful writer. I write the words upon the tablet of my heart.

My heart is stirred by a noble theme, as I recite my verses for the King.

The Holy Spirit is my teacher and guide. He reveals the Word to me so that I can understand it.

I have been enriched in all my knowledge and in all my speech.

I do not put out the Spirit's fire. In fact, I fan into flame the gift of God which is in me.

I have the spirit of revelation and knowledge. I am coming to know Christ better every day.

I have the glorious inheritance working inside of me.

I have the same power of God that was used to raise Christ from the dead. I have resurrection power within me.

I cast my cares upon the Lord, because He cares for me and watches over me affectionately. He has my best interest at heart.

I hunger for righteousness. I am filled with all the spiritual blessings in heavenly places.

I meditate in the Word day and night, so that I can recognize God's will and then act upon it. As I practice the Word, I am blessed in everything I do.

Chapter 2

Positive Confessions Can Fail

There is an interesting verse in the Bible that I came across which explains why Jesus' words always came to pass.

You say, "His words always came to pass because He is the Son of God." But that's only part of the truth. The following Scripture explains why Jesus' words always came to pass: "For the one whom God sent speaks the words of God, for God gives the Spirit without limit" (John 3:34).

Notice that Jesus had the Spirit "without limit." And why did God give Him the Spirit without limit? Many think it was because Jesus was the Son of God, so only He could have the Spirit without limit. But look at the Scripture carefully.

It says, "For the one whom God sent speaks the words of God..." There are two reasons that Jesus had the Spirit without measure: first, because He was the Son of God; second, because He so valued God's words that He refused to speak anything which was contrary to God's revealed will. He only spoke God's words.

God will turn up the power in your life if you speak only according to God's words. If much of what you say is contrary to God's words, God will lower the power of your words in order to protect you from getting bad things. But by doing this, you also are kept from receiving many good things.

However, if you will speak only God's words, then God can trust you, so He will turn up the power of your words. When He does, you will receive more of what you say.

Value Your Words

"The tongue has the power of life and death, and those who love it will eat its fruit" (Prov. 18:21). **Those who love it** will eat its fruit. Did you get that?

I've read this Scripture literally hundreds of times, yet one day I saw it. I realized that only **those who love it** will eat its fruit.

Love what? Love "it." What is "it"? "It" is "words." So basically, those who love, appreciate, and value their words will eat its fruit.

Do you see the trouble with most of us? We don't love, appreciate, and value our words and, more importantly, we don't value God's Word. Consequently, we don't eat the good fruit of our words. We, too often, don't value the power of the spoken Word of God. This is why our words often don't come to pass.

If you don't esteem your words and see them as being highly important, then most likely you are not going to eat much fruit from them.

You might say, "I don't believe in that confession stuff. It doesn't work for me!" Of course it doesn't, because you don't esteem the biblical principle of the confession of God's Word. Confession worked for Jesus, because He valued the power of the spoken Word. When He said, "Be healed!" the people were healed. When He said to a dead man, "Lazarus, come forth!" the dead man came forth.

Jesus received everything He said, because He placed tremendous importance on His words and He also respected God's words as being the final authority in His life. He refused to say anything that would disrespect God's authority.

Positive confession has not worked for many people because they don't value the spoken Word. They have used the teaching on faith and positive confession as a gimmick to get what they wanted, rather than looking at it as a way of life.

Many times people try to apply the message of faith when they are going through a great trial, yet they only understand the method of confession, not the principle of confession.

Any parrot can repeat words: "I'm healed, I'm blessed, I'm a conqueror." But we are not parrots. We must understand the principle of confession. Know the principle of confession, and you will understand why confession works and how it works.

Magic or Miracle

When I first heard a preacher teach on confession, he made a big deal out of something that I realized later was not a big deal. He said, "Don't ever say, 'I'm tickled pink' because you may get it." How silly! You are not going to turn pink for saying those words. It is statements like that which have hurt the message of **faith and confession**.

I'm sure that this teacher meant well. He was trying to get us to avoid negative talk. He was showing that we have perverted the healing power in humor.

The Bible says, "A merry heart does good, like medicine" (Prov. 17:22 NKJV). Laughter is the best medicine. This teacher was right! We have perverted the healing power of humor. In connection with humor, we say, "I laughed so hard that I thought I was going to bust a gut!" "I died laughing!" "That comedian cracks me up!" "I exploded with laughter." Notice that we use such violent terms to speak of laughter: "Bust a gut!" "Died laughing! "Cracks me up!" "Exploded with laughter!"

This preacher rightly pointed these things out, but then he said, "Don't say, 'I was tickled pink' because you may get it." You are not going to turn pink for saying that. Why aren't you? Because you don't believe you will. Words alone don't have power; it is the faith in those words which has power.

Faith in Words

The most famous passage in the Bible concerning the power of faith's confessions is when Jesus said,

> *For verily I say unto you, That whosoever shall say unto this mountain, Be*

> *thou removed, and be thou cast into the*
> *sea; and shall not doubt in his heart, but*
> *shall believe that those things which he*
> *saith shall come to pass; he shall have*
> *whatsoever he saith.* (Mark 11:23 KJV)

Jesus said that if you believe that what you say will come to pass, you will have whatever you say.

What did Jesus say that you'll have? Not what you "say." People teach that you will have what you say, but that is simply part of the truth. The whole truth is that you'll have what you "believe" that you are saying. You have to believe that your words will come to pass. If you simply speak something that you don't believe will happen, then there is no spiritual force in your words. Your words will likely fail to produce, whether they were good or bad.

Have you heard the story of the man who learned about speaking to mountains and moving them by words? In his back yard there was a small hill, so he thought that he would try this "faith stuff." He said out loud to the hill, "I command you to leave my back yard and go into the sea."

The next morning, he woke up and immediately looked in his backyard. To his dismay, the hill was still there. He exclaimed, "I knew that it wouldn't work!"

This is the way many approach the message of faith. They try it out to see if it will work, but they don't really believe that it will. When it does not work, they tell everyone, "I tried that message of faith, and it doesn't work. So don't even bother to try it."

The trouble with them is that they didn't have faith. Faith can only work where there is faith. That sounds obvious, but many miss this simple truth. Faith is being fully convinced or deeply persuaded that something is true. So before your words can be powerful, your heart must believe. And this kind of faith will only come through the revelation of the Holy Spirit and your meditation on that revelation.

Mouth and Heart Must Agree

There is a connection between the power of your words and the conviction of your heart. This is what the apostle Paul meant when he wrote the two steps for salvation.

But what does it say? "The word is near you; it is in your mouth and in your heart," that is, the word of faith we are proclaiming: That if you confess with

your mouth, "Jesus is Lord," and believe
in your heart that God raised him from
the dead, you will be saved. For it is
with your heart that you believe and are
justified, and it is with your mouth that
you confess and are saved.

(Rom. 10:8–10)

The two steps which anyone can take that
will cause him to be saved are: **believe** in your
heart that Jesus rose from the dead and **confess** with your **mouth** that Jesus is Lord. You
can easily see the connection between the
mouth and the heart. It is not only confessing
that brings salvation into your life, but also
believing with your heart. Jesus will not become your Lord through confession only. You
must also believe. This is true in every realm
of receiving from God.

If all you do is confess your healing or
prosperity or any other blessing promised in
God's Word, but do not truly believe, then your
confession will not work. You know whether or
not you truly believe.

When I speak of "believing," I do not mean
simply "mentally agreeing." Anyone can mentally agree to certain truths, but never truly
believe. True faith is in the heart, not in the
head.

For example, many reading this book have always believed in their minds that Jesus is the Son of God and that He died for their sins, but believing that did not save them. It was only when their faith traveled from their heads into their hearts that they were saved.

Many religious people believe correctly concerning Jesus dying for their sins and rising from the dead. They even confess these things in their creeds. Yet many of them are not saved because they believe with their heads only and not with their hearts.

I've written all this to show why confession may not work at times. You can say all the right things—"I'm healed, I'm blessed"—but still not receive, because you don't have real faith in what you are confessing. You may simply be saying what you've been trained to say. However, faith does not come through training but through revelation by studying the Word.

You Can Predict Your Future
by saying...

I esteem my words and treat them with respect. More than that, I esteem God and His Word above everything.

My words are increasing in power and force, because I let nothing come out of my mouth except what is helpful in building up others according to their needs.

I love my words. I reap my words. My words are working to produce life.

The Spirit is turning up the power of my words, because I speak God's words.

God's Word is the final authority in my life. I do not accept anything that does not line up with God's Word.

I reject all tradition that does not conform to God's Word.

I refuse to say anything that would disrespect God's authority.

I have a merry heart, and it does good like medicine.

I am more than a conqueror through Christ who loves me.

I have faith in my words. I believe what I say comes to pass.

The Word is near me. It is in my mouth and in my heart. It is the word of faith that I proclaim.

Chapter 3

Why Words Are Powerful

Many people, when they first hear about the power of words, think that this teaching sounds superstitious. They contend that anyone who believes in the power of words is irrational. They scoff, "You have to be ignorant to believe that what you say can come to pass."

These people are right, if there is no God then words mean nothing. But there is a God, and, most significantly, He cares about us and is active in our lives. But He also demands that we cooperate with Him in determining our destiny by confessing His Word. God works by means of His Word, and His Word is spoken through people.

Paul writes, "And we also thank God continually because, when you received the word of God, which you heard from us, you accepted it not as the word of men"(1 Thess. 2:13). Notice, this church heard the Word of God from the apostles. They did not hear the Word thundered from heaven or spoken by an angel. God rarely chooses to speak His Word that way, but instead, loves to speak it through human beings.

You may want to argue with this and say, "God can do anything He wants to, with or without us." This is true—God can do anything. However, He has chosen to work through people. This is God's prerogative. If He wanted to work apart from mankind, then He could. But He has chosen to work through men. The quicker we accept this, the better we can cooperate with God.

Remember, "we are God's fellow workers" (1 Cor. 3:9). We have our part to play in the divine out-working of God's will for our lives.

In God's Image

Not only does God want to work through us, but He has created us in such a way that He can work through us. He created us in His image in order that He may work through us. By making us into His image, God gave us the capacity to operate in His divine power. Let's understand clearly what it means to be created in God's image and how this relates to the power of the spoken Word.

> *Then God said, "Let us make man in our image, in our likeness, and let them rule over the fish of the sea and the birds of the air, over the livestock, over all the earth, and over all the creatures that move along the ground." So God created man in his own image, in the image of God he created him; male and female he created them.* (Gen. 1:26–27)

Who is God speaking to when He said, "Let **us**"? The pronoun "us" is plural. This implies that there is more to God than "one." Yet the Bible says that there is only "one" God. So how could God refer to Himself as "us?"

The answer is simple; The Trinity is talking. The Father and Son and Holy Spirit, in choir-like voices, sing, "Let us make man in our image, in our likeness." The entire Trinity was involved in creation, especially in the creation of mankind. This makes Their statement about the creation of mankind extremely important.

And what did the Trinity say regarding the creation of mankind? They said, "Let us make man in our image and our likeness." God made man in His image and likeness by breathing into him the breath of life.

> *The LORD God formed the man from the dust of the ground and breathed into his nostrils the breath of life, and the man became a living being* [spirit]. *(Gen. 2:7)*

Our bodies are made of the same stuff that the animal bodies are made of, but we are also different from the animals because God personally breathed His own life into us, thereby, creating us in His image.

People erroneously think that man was created out of dust, but this is not true. To create something is to make something out of nothing. However, man's body is **formed** from dust. To form something implies taking something that already exists and then gradually shaping it into something, much like a potter does to a lump of clay. Dust already existed. Man's body is from something that already existed. Our bodies come from the same stuff of the animals—dust.

Unfortunately, this is the only thing scientists study. They simply study what can be seen, like our bodies. They also study the animals and discover that we are not too different from the animals. Some scientists even call us animals—just a highly evolved species. They arrive at their conclusion by physical evidence only.

Yet, the Bible tells us something else about mankind. It does say that the body is made from the same stuff as the animals, but it also says that mankind has something else that the animals do not have, and that's a spirit.

Man's spirit is the creation of God. Creation is to take something that does not exist and cause it to exist. Mankind is created from God's breath—His Spirit. This creation of man's spirit took place instantly. Man's body was formed first, afterward his spirit was created.

God did not create the body; instead, He formed it. He created the human spirit, though. So creation is not the body, but the human spirit. Man was made in God's image the moment God breathed a spirit into him.

Jesus said, "God is spirit" (John 4:24). Since man is in the image of God, this means that man is a spirit. Man can act like God, because he, too, is a spirit. This does not mean that man is God, but rather, that man can act like God as far as is humanly possible.

"Be imitators of God, therefore, as dearly loved children" (Eph. 5:1). God wants us to imitate Him in every respect that is possible for creatures. God is the Creator; we are creatures. Therefore, we can never imitate God in the exact fashion of God, but we can imitate Him as far as is possible for human beings.

Words Are Spiritual Forces

You might say to me, "Tom, what does all this have to do with the power of words?" The moment that God breathed into man His own life and gave man a spirit, the man was able to speak. Intelligent communication is what separates us from the animals, and it is also what unites us with God. The ability to speak shows that we are in God's image.

If you look at the story in Genesis, you will notice that the first job which God gave man was to name the animals. To name the animals requires speech. Man's first job was to talk.

Notice that God gave man the responsibility to name the animals. God could have, if He wanted to, name the animals Himself, but instead, He preferred to let Adam work with Him in determining the destiny of the world. God made the world, then gave Adam dominion over it. "Let them have dominion" (Gen. 1:26 KJV).

The way Adam would exercise dominion over this world was through the God-like ability of speech. This ability of speech comes from man's spirit. We have the ability to speak because we have a spirit. Actually, man is a spirit. The human spirit is what enables us to speak. It is not the shape of the jaw or any other natural phenomenon that makes us talk. It is our spirit that gives us the power to speak.

The reason our words are so powerful is because they are spiritual forces. They are not simply sound waves. Sound waves are not powerful. Spirit is powerful. Jesus said, "The words I have spoken to you are spirit and they are life" (John 6:63). Words are spirit, and that is what makes them powerful.

God's Word Works Wonders

Look at how God created the universe. He created everything with words. In Genesis chapter one, verses 3, 6, 9, 14, 20, 24, and 26, we find the same phrase used over and over again: "And God said!" "And God said!" "And God said!" God created everything by speaking it into existence.

It seems rather redundant for Moses, the author of Genesis, to keep saying, "And God said," before every aspect of creation. If Moses would have had to send the book of Genesis to an editor, the editor would have changed the wording to, "And God said, Let there be light, sky, land, water, plants, sun, moon, stars, fish, birds, animals, and man." The editor would have condensed the creation account, but by doing that, he would have ruined the impact which God intended to make.

By repetition God was emphasizing how He made everything, not simply that He did make everything. *How* He made everything is very important. How did God make everything? By words! The Hebrew writer emphasizes this point:

> *By faith we understand that the universe was formed at God's command, so that what is seen was not made out of what was visible.* *(Heb. 11:3)*

We see from this Scripture that words—God's words—created the entire universe. God said it, and it came to be. This planet is here because of God's Word. The sun is here because of God's Word. The moon is here because of God's Word. The stars are here because of God's Word. He spoke the entire universe into being!

Since God is able to create things by words, we can create things by words because we are in His image. This is how God intended it to be. God creates by words, so man creates by words. But the words that we are called to speak are God's words, not our own words.

You Can Predict Your Future
by saying...

I have been created in God's image. I am a spirit, I have a soul, and I live in a body.

God has given me dominion. I have the power and right to govern and control.

My words are spirit, and they are life.

My first job is to cooperate with God in naming the kind of life I will have.

God's Word is not void of power. It has the ability within itself to reproduce. I make God's Word my words.

I have been made complete in Him. I am growing up in my salvation. My faith is growing exceedingly.

God is faithful. What He said, He is able to bring to pass.

God's Word comes out of my mouth, and it accomplishes what God desires and achieves the purpose for which He sent it.

I desire to please my heavenly Father by imitating Him.

I will walk in love and walk by faith in God's Word.

Chapter 4

Beyond God's Word

T he problem with the people of Babel was that they wanted to speak their own words, not God's words. The story of Babel begins by revealing that the whole world spoke the same way. "Now the whole world had one language and a common speech" (Gen. 11:1). And what did the whole world declare? "They said to each other, 'Come, let's make bricks...Come, let us build ourselves a city'" (Gen. 11:3–4).

They used the same phrase that God used to create mankind: "Let us!" That's exactly the phrase God used. The people of Babel were imitating God, not as "dearly loved children," but rather as selfish, egotistical brats.

Nevertheless, what is amazing is that God believed their words had the power to come to pass. Listen to what God said.

> *The LORD said, "If as one people speaking the same language they have begun to do this, then nothing they plan to do will be impossible for them." (Gen.11:6)*

God knows the power of words. He declared that nothing was impossible for them because they were speaking in unity. Jesus said, "Everything is possible for him who believes" (Mark 9:23). This is true even for people who did not consider God. Even the words of sinners are powerful. How much more powerful should our words be as saints of God?

The real power of the people of Babel lies in their words. Their words created within them the power, wisdom, and organization necessary to build a city. Without their words, they were powerless. This is why God confused their language. Without a common language, God knew that they would never have the power to complete their goal. God confused their language by His own Word. "Come, let us go down and confuse their language" (Gen. 11:7).

God used the same phrase that the people copied from Him: "**Let Us.**" God's Word is ultimately much more powerful than the words of people. God's words overruled their words. God is sovereign and can overrule any words that people speak.

The lesson we learn is that we should imitate God as dearly loved children by speaking according to His will and purpose, which are laid out in His Word. We should not use the power of confession as selfish brats, but as loving children who want to please our heavenly Father.

Worldly Words

The world, like Babylon, has understood the power of words. This is why there are many self-help books on the market aimed toward the non-believer. Many of these books discuss the power of words; they even provide "positive confessions" for their readers to use. They often call these confessions such things as "self-talk," "daily affirmations," or "power words." The world has become like Babylon: people use the method of "positive confessions" to get what they want instead of submitting themselves to the will of God. Christians have sometimes acted like Babylonians as well.

Because of the modern Babylonian gurus, many Christians, in order to disassociate themselves from them, will be afraid to speak things into existence. They think that by doing this, they are participating in witchcraft, mind-over-matter, sorcery, or magic. And, of course, there are many cult-watchers who see demons behind every bush. If someone like myself teaches on the power of words, then these heresy hunters come out of the bushes to exclaim, "This teaching is 'new age' doctrine!"

Well, I refuse to surrender the truths of the Bible to the charlatans. Just because some false leader teaches biblical truths in a twisted manner does not mean that biblical truths are to be abandoned. This is what many Christians have done. They have handed over biblical truths to the devil's counterfeiters. This is just as foolish to do as it would be for the United States to quit making money just because counterfeiters do.

I am often asked by paranoid cult-watchers, "Do you believe in positive confession?"

I answer them, "No! I believe in the positive confession **of God's Word**!" You see, it is not simply "positive confession" that is powerful. It is the confession of "God's Word" that is powerful! I don't believe in speaking just anything and therefore thinking that it is going to come to pass. No, I believe in speaking God's Word. God's Word is what is powerful, not my word.

Someone might say, "If I confessed that I was going to be a millionaire, do you think I would become one?" First of all, why would you confess that you are going to be a millionaire?

"Because I want to be one."

Fine, but where in the Bible does God promise to make you a millionaire? Nowhere. God does not promise to make you a millionaire, so don't bother to confess it, unless, of course, God gave you a special revelation that He wanted you to become a millionaire. In that case, it would be all right. But, if God hasn't given you that revelation, then simply speak what He has promised you.

He has promised to supply all your needs, "And my God will meet all your needs according to his glorious riches in Christ Jesus" (Phil. 4:19). So put that promise in your mouth. Confess, "My God shall supply all my needs according to God's riches in glory by Christ Jesus." Now you are confessing God's Word. That Word is imperishable and incorruptible. However, saying that you are going to be a millionaire is like planting perishable seed—most likely it will not come to pass.

God promises to supply all your need, not all your greed. He does not promise to supply a Lexus for you. Now, He may want you to have a Lexus, so if He does, go ahead and confess one. Yet many confess, "I have a Lexus or Cadillac or some other great luxury automobile," but they haven't learned to appreciate what they do have.

There was a time when I was driving a very old 1974 Matador. It used to be a health department car. It still had the health insignia on it when I drove it. It was an embarrassment to drive this car to church and preach on prosperity. Because of my frustration with this car, I would complain to others about how bad this car was. Then I would add, "However, I am trusting God for a new one." It seemed to take forever to get enough money to buy a better car, so I really took the matter to God in prayer.

As I was in prayer for a new car the Lord said to me, "If you'll start to appreciate and speak well of your car, instead of complaining, I'll give you something better." I was quick to repent. At that moment I started to appreciate my 1974 Matador. Soon I had enough money to buy a better car.

Many greedy Christians have hurt the message of Bible prosperity. They focus on confessing a new car or new house, but miss what the entire Bible says about prosperity.

You see, we should not go beyond the Bible in our confession but stay within the

Scriptures. When we advance beyond the Word in our confession, we often don't receive what we confess and, worst of all, we shipwreck our faith.

For example, some confess, "I'm okay, you're okay!" They think that these words are going to come to pass, but they are wrong because God does not say, "I'm okay, you're okay." Those words are not found in the Scriptures.

The Bible does say, "[God] who began a good work in you will carry it on to completion until the day of Christ Jesus" (Phil. 1:6). Confessing those words is a whole lot better than confessing the words, "I'm okay, you're okay."

There is a great example in the New Testament which shows that it is all right to make a positive confession based on God's Word.

> *Keep your lives free from the love of money and be content with what you have, because God has said, "Never will I leave you and never will I forsake you." So we say with confidence, "The Lord is my helper; I will not be afraid. What can man do to me?"* (Heb. 13:5–6)

Notice that the writer of Hebrews took verse six from Psalm 118, which is a statement that God said to David, and applied it to the church. He then says, "Because God has said...So we say with confidence." We can say because God has first said. This is true biblical confession; it is simply saying what God has already said.

True biblical confession is finding Bible verses that promise certain things—like health, prosperity, mental wholeness—and then appropriating them to our case by confessing them. Doing this is thoroughly scriptural and has nothing to do with metaphysical practice. It also keeps us within scriptural bounds and makes our words imperishable.

So you have a choice whether to plant perishable or imperishable seed. Choose to plant the imperishable seed, which is God's Word, and it will always come to pass.

You Can Predict Your Future
by saying...

I do not go beyond God's Word. I speak not worldly words, but I speak godly words.

Whatever is of a good report, I speak it and think it.

My God shall supply all of my needs according to His riches in glory by Christ Jesus.

He is my shepherd, so I don't have a care in the world.

I can say what God has said. Because He has said, "Never will I leave you and never will I forsake you," I can say with boldness, "The Lord is my helper; I will not be afraid. What can man do to me?"

Chapter 5

Incorruptible Seed

We have all heard the story of Mary and the angel Gabriel. However, what hasn't been told enough is how the miracle of the virgin birth took place.

The angel declared to Mary that she would be "with child" and give birth to a son and name Him Jesus. Mary asked how this could be since she was a virgin.

The angel answered that the Holy Spirit was going to overshadow her so that the one conceived in her would be the Son of God. This sounds impossible, doesn't it? Because of the impossibility of a virgin birth, the angel said, "For nothing is impossible with God" (Luke 1:37). The literal Greek text says, "For no word from God is void of power."

God's Word is not void of power; man's word is void of power. You see, the thing that

55

makes all things possible is God's Word. Without His Word, nothing is possible.

God sent the angel Gabriel to give the "good news" to Mary (Luke 1:19). God didn't simply surprise Mary with the virgin birth, because He knows that the impossible can only be possible when people receive the Word of God. He sent the angel to give Mary this word.

Mary made a very important statement which shows how she was able to conceive the Son of God. She said, "I am the Lord's servant. May it be to me as you have said" (Luke 1:38). Mary believed the word that God spoke through the angel. Consequently, that word was planted in her spirit until it became flesh.

This is how it works for us. We hear God's Word through the Bible. The Holy Spirit overshadows us and gives us revelation of the Word. When we meditate on that Word, it enters our spirits until it becomes absolutely real to us. Finally, after a period of time, the Word materializes. This can only work when we receive God's Word.

If we receive man's words, then our faith is only as powerful as human words. Since we have discovered that man's words have lost the original power that they had before the Fall, we should not put our trust in man's words—and that includes our own words.

Make God's Seed Yours

If our words have lost much of the original power that they had before the Fall, what would be the most logical thing to do? The best thing to do would be to speak God's words. God's words are still as powerful as ever. It is man's words that have lost the power, not God's words. "For you have been born again, not of perishable seed, but of imperishable, through the living and enduring word of God" (1 Pet. 1:23). Peter calls God's Word "imperishable seed," while man's words are "perishable seed."

"Imperishable" means incapable of dying. Every word that God speaks is alive. No word from God is dead. "For the word of God is living and active" (Heb. 4:12).

I have planted many things in my life including flowers and trees. In my experience, some of the things I planted grew, and some did not grow at all; some grew at the beginning and died later. Everything did not grow perfectly, because natural seeds are perishable. Some seeds produce; some don't. Words are like that. Some are good and produce fruit; others are bad and are forgotten. Some of the things we say come to pass, while other things do not.

The reason is simple: words are perishable or subject to death. Everything in this world is subject to death, including words. This is why your words can fail to come to pass.

There is only one thing in this world that is imperishable—the Word of God. God's Word is imperishable seed. It will come to pass all of the time. It is scriptural and proper for believers to take promises in the Old Testament and apply them to their life today, because "No matter how many promises God has made, they are 'Yes' in Christ" (2 Cor. 1:20).

So, instead of speaking the words that come from your head, you should speak the words that come from God's head. This is what God meant for you to do when He said, "For my thoughts are not your thoughts, neither are your ways my ways" (Isa. 55:8). He then went on to say, "So is my word that goes out from my mouth: It will not return to me empty, but will accomplish what I desire and achieve the purpose for which I sent it" (Isa. 55:11).

God tells you not to speak what comes from your thoughts, but to speak what comes from His thoughts, because your thoughts are so limited and impotent. If we speak our thoughts, dreams, and hopes without discovering God's Word, then we will probably fail to receive them because our words are weak and perishable. So God tells us to speak His Word instead of our words, so that it will "accomplish" and "achieve" the purpose for which God sent it.

God sent His Word so that we could have something imperishable to count on. Our thoughts and words cannot be trusted, but God's words can!

You Can Predict Your Future
by saying...

All things are possible with God, and I choose to believe in Him.

The world may trust in horses and chariots, but I trust in the name of the Lord.

His name is a strong tower; I run to it and am safe.

Like Mary, I receive God's Word inside my heart, I meditate on it, and it becomes flesh.

I will not speak what comes to my mind but will speak what is in God's mind.

God's Word will not return to Him void, but will accomplish what He desires and achieve the purpose for which He sent it.

I plant the imperishable Word of God into my life and into others. It never fails to produce.

I can trust in God's Word because it is impossible for God to lie. Let every man be a liar, and let God be true.

Chapter 6

Prophesy Your Future

*Having then gifts differing
according to the grace that is
given to us, whether prophecy, let
us prophesy according to the
proportion of faith.*
—Romans 12:6 KJV

Prophesy means to foretell—to predict the future. In this Scripture it says, "Let us prophesy according to the proportion of faith." You can predict the future according to the level of your faith.

The word "prophesy" is the Greek word *prophemi*. It is a compound of two words: *pro* which means "before" and *phemi* which means "to speak." Put them together, and it means "to speak before it happens."

The interesting part of this word is *phemi*. The counterpart to *phemi* is *rhema*. *Rhema* is the Greek word for "the spoken word of God."

So, literally, this word means to "speak forth the future by speaking the word of God." You can predict your future by prophesying the Word of God. To prophesy is to speak forth the Word of God so that you can predict your future.

The Bible mentions two kinds of prophecy: causative and noncausative. The kind that most are familiar with is noncausative prophesy. It is inspired utterance about what will take place in the future. This type of prophesy does not make things come to pass; it only reveals what will come to pass.

Let me give you an illustration. A meteorologist (weather man) predicts the weather. He may say that it will be warm and sunny. If it happens, we don't credit him with the good weather. If he predicts that there will be a tornado and it happens, we don't get mad at him, because he is not the cause of the bad weather nor is he the cause of the good weather. This is a type of noncausative prophecy. It does not cause the weather.

Causative Prophesy in Action

The prophets in the Bible predicted the future. They knew what the future was going to be like based on divine revelation, so they simply said what was going to happen, and it did. Many of their prophecies were noncausative. Their prophecies did not make the bad things happen, nor did they cause the good things to happen.

However, some of their prophecies were causative. That is, their prophecies made things happen. Let me show you an example of causative prophecy.

> *The hand of the LORD was upon me, and he brought me out by the Spirit of the LORD and set me in the middle of a valley; it was full of bones. He led me back and forth among them, and I saw a great many bones on the floor of the valley; bones that were very dry. He asked me, "Son of man, can these bones live?" I said, "O Sovereign LORD, you alone know." Then he said to me, "Prophesy to these bones and say to them, 'Dry bones, hear the word of the LORD! This is what the Sovereign LORD says to these bones: I will make breath enter you, and you will come to life. I will attach tendons to you and make flesh come upon you and cover you with skin; I will put breath in you, and you will come to life. Then you will know that I am the LORD.'" So I prophesied as I was commanded. And as*

> *I was prophesying, there was a noise, a*
> *rattling sound, and the bones came to-*
> *gether, bone to bone.*   *(Ezek. 37:1–7)*

You see, as Ezekiel prophesied, the bones came together. As long as he was silent, nothing happened. If he would have waited for God to do something, the bones would not have joined together. Ezekiel's prophecy caused the bones to unite.

> *Then he said to me, "Prophesy to the*
> *breath; prophesy, son of man, and say to*
> *it, 'This is what the Sovereign LORD*
> *says: Come from the four winds, O*
> *breath, and breathe into these slain, that*
> *they may live.'" So I prophesied as he*
> *commanded me, and breath entered*
> *them; they came to life and stood up on*
> *their feet—a vast army..."Therefore*
> *prophesy and say to them: 'This is what*
> *the Sovereign LORD says: O my people, I*
> *am going to open your graves and bring*
> *you up from them; I will bring you back*
> *to the land of Israel.'" (Ezek. 37:9–10, 12)*

Please notice that when God asked Ezekiel if he thought that the bones could live, he answered that only God knew. But God was not satisfied with his answer, so He told him to prophesy life to the bones, which, of course, let Ezekiel know that it was God's will for the bones to come to life and, most importantly, Ezekiel would be instrumental in making it happen.

This brings us to something very important in our own lives. God will ask a sick person, "Can you be healed?" And often he answers, "Only you know, Lord!" Then he stops with that answer. Unfortunately, often a Christian is not familiar enough with the Word to be able to hear God telling him to prophesy his healing by saying, "I am healed by the stripes of Jesus. I forbid sickness to touch my body. I am redeemed from the curse of sickness. So, devil, be gone!" Pitifully, the sick person usually answers, "Only the Lord knows if I'm going to be healed. It's up to Him to heal me. If He wants me well, He will heal me. If He doesn't, then He won't heal me." Wrong!

Ezekiel did not have that passive attitude. Once he heard God's Word concerning the dry bones, he knew God's will. He also knew that he had a part in bringing God's will to pass. His part was to prophesy. To prophesy is to speak forth the future by using the Word of God. Only when Ezekiel prophesied did the bones come to life. If he would have waited for God to do something, then the bones would have stayed dead. Ezekiel prophesied the bones to life!

Are you prophesying your bones to life? Some are saying, "I'm sure getting old. I can't get around like I used to. My bones are getting brittle. I can hardly walk. I guess I'm going to have to use a cane soon."

Do you know what they are doing? They are prophesying death to their bones!

"But, Tom, we all have to get old!" you might say.

Yes, we are getting older, but we don't have to get frail and sick. We can be like Moses. The Bible says, "Moses was a hundred and twenty years old when he died, yet his eyes were not weak nor his strength gone" (Deut. 34:7). Go ahead and prophesy death, weakness and premature aging if you want to, but I'm prophesying life, strength, and vigor. I'm going to get what I'm prophesying—and so are you!

You are only as young as your confession. My favorite Scripture that makes me stay young is Psalm 103:5 (KJV), "Who satisfieth thy mouth with good *things; so that* thy youth is renewed like the eagle's."

Notice that God "satisfieth thy mouth with good things." Why does He satisfy "thy mouth with good things"? The answer is "so that thy youth is renewed like the eagle's."

Is your mouth satisfied with the good things of God's Word? Do you love to speak God's good Word over your life? If you do, then your youth will be renewed like the eagle's! Your words can make you age prematurely or they can renew your youth! I use my words to renew my youth.

Except at My Word

Let us look at another example of causative prophecy.

> *Now Elijah the Tishbite, from Tishbe in Gilead, said to Ahab, "As the LORD, the God of Israel, lives, whom I serve, there will be neither dew nor rain in the next few years except at my word."*
>
> *(1 Kings 17:1)*

At this time in history, the nation of Israel was backslidden. They were disobedient to God. They had started making idols and were worshipping them. Yet, in all of this, they were not experiencing any trouble.

This surprised Elijah, because he knew that Deuteronomy said that if they ever turned away from God, "The LORD would turn the rain of their country into dust and powder" (v. 28:24).

Yet, even though Israel had disobeyed the Law, they were not experiencing drought. God said that if they disobeyed Him they would have drought, but they were not having drought. Why was there not drought in the land? There was no drought because no one up to that time had prophesied that word from Deuteronomy 28:24.

So Elijah pronounced the curse over Israel based on the Word of God in Deuteronomy 28:24. He said, "There will be neither dew nor rain in the next few years except at my word" (1 Kings 17:1).

Notice that Elijah did not say, "Except at God's word." He said, "Except at my word." Elijah was bold to link God's Word with his own. This is what prophecy is all about. It is linking God's Word with your word and speaking it forth in order to predict the future. Elijah predicted Israel's future by prophesying God's Word.

Elijah prophesied the curse because Israel was under the curse. How does the curse affect us today? Galatians 3:13 says, "Christ redeemed us from the curse of the law." We are not under the curse, so we don't have to curse our lives. We can bless our lives because the blessings of Abraham are ours! We can prophesy the blessings of Abraham—healing, favor, peace, prosperity, victory, and a whole lot more!

According to the Measure of Faith

Remember Romans 12:6 (KJV) says, "*Let us prophesy* according to the proportion of faith!" You cannot prophesy beyond your level of faith. Since faith comes by hearing God's Word, you can only prophesy according to what you have been hearing.

This is why Elijah, three and a half years later, went onto Mount Carmel. Israel had repented, so Elijah knew that it was time for Israel to be blessed again. Unfortunately, he was accustomed to the curse. He did not have complete faith that Israel would be blessed again, so he went on top of the mountain to hear from God. When he reached the top of the mountain, he got on his knees and put his head between his legs.

Because of the Spirit and the Word working in his heart to give him revelation, he said, "There is the sound of a heavy rain" (1 Kings 18:41). He told his servant, "Go and look toward the sea" (1 Kings 18:43). The servant did as Elijah told him. He came back and reported, "'There is nothing there'...Seven times Elijah said, 'Go back'" (v. 43).

In my mind's eye, I can picture the servant's eyebrow curl. He must have thought, "Something's wrong with my master. He is hearing things." But he did as he was told. "Sorry, master. There is nothing there."

"Go back." Elijah continued to shout. He did this seven times. And on the seventh time, the servant saw a little cloud. Should he say something or not about this insignificant cloud? After all, he didn't want to get the prophet's hopes up. However, he opened his mouth, "A cloud as small as a man's hand is rising from the sea" (1 Kings 18:44).

Fire lit the prophet's eyes, and he said, "Go tell Ahab, 'Hitch up your chariot and go down before the rain stops you'" (v. 44).

Before the servant could give the good news, a heavy rain came on the land. God had blessed Israel again.

Why did Elijah climb the mountain? He did it because he wanted to get alone with God in prayer so that God could speak to him. The word which God gave Elijah was "a heavy rain" (1 Kings 18:41). Elijah kept hearing that word over and over again until it got down into his spirit. When it did, he had faith to prophesy. He prophesied according to the measure of faith as Romans 12:6 says.

You, too, can prophesy the Word of God according to the measure of your faith. What are you hearing from God? You should be hearing His Word which says...

No weapon forged against you will prevail.   *(Isa. 54:17)*

The one who is in you is greater than the one who is in the world.   *(1 John 4:4)*

In all these things we are more than conquerors through him who loved us.
(Rom. 8:37)

With God all things are possible.
(Matt. 19:26)

I can do everything through him who gives me strength.   *(Phil. 4:13)*

Who is it that overcomes the world? Only he who believes that Jesus is the Son of God.   *(1 John 5:5)*

If anyone is in Christ, he is a new creation; the old has gone, the new has come!
(2 Cor. 5:17)

*Submit yourselves, then, to God. Resist
the devil, and he will flee from you.*
(James 4:7)

If God is for us, who can be against us?
(Rom. 8:31)

Prophesy the blessings of God in your life.
Prophesy according to the measure of your
faith. Prophesy what you believe God can and
will do for you!

You Can Predict Your Future
by saying...

I prophesy according to the measure of
faith within me. I take God's Word and speak
in out of my mouth before it happens.

My faith comes by hearing as I listen to
the Word of God.

The hand of the Lord is upon me. As I
prophesy, great things happen.

I am a vessel for the Lord. He uses me as
He sees fit. He is the potter, and I am the clay.

Though the outward man is decaying, my
inward man is being renewed day by day.

My youth is renewed like the eagle's. Like
Moses, my eyes are not growing dim nor is my
strength gone.

I do not forget any of the Lord's benefits. He forgives all my iniquities, and He heals all my diseases. He satisfies my desires with good things. He redeems my life from the pit and crowns me with love and compassion.

God works through my words.

I release Christ in me, the hope of glory.

I hear the sound of an abundance of blessings. It is coming my way! Glory be to God!

Chapter 7

Chart Your Course

Job 22:28 says, in the Amplified version, "You shall also decide *and* decree a thing, and it shall be established for you, and the light [of God's favor] shall shine upon your ways."

God says to decide and decree a thing, and you'll get it. We must do more than "decide"; we must "**decree**."

A decree is a proclamation made by someone with authority. A decree is always made by kings. A king makes a decree by declaring what is legal and what is illegal, and everyone has to obey it. His words are law. His words determine the future of his domain.

For if, by the trespass of the one man, death reigned through that one man, how much more will those who receive

God's abundant provision of grace and
of the gift of righteousness reign in life
through the one man, Jesus Christ.

(Rom. 5:17)

You are meant to reign in life through Jesus Christ. The same Scripture in the Amplified Bible says, "Those who receive [God's]
overflowing grace (unmerited favor) and the
free gift of righteousness...reign as kings in
life..." You can reign as a king, because you are
a king.

Revelation 1:6 (KJV) says, "And [Jesus]
hath made us kings and priests unto God and
his Father." What has Jesus made us? Kings
and priests.

Thank God for the Protestant Reforma-
tion, because it brought us the truth of the
priesthood of every believer. However, it ne-
glected the revelation of the kingly authority
of every believer. Thank God that we are
kings!

You might want to pause for a moment
and declare, "I am a king!" You might say,
"But I don't feel like a king." Well, what do
feelings have to do with anything? Anyway,
what does a king feel like?

"Well, I think I would feel better than
this," you might say.

Let me ask you something. Are you saved? Are you a new creature in Christ Jesus? Of course you are!

Do you always feel saved? Do you always feel like a new creature? Of course not, yet you are one anyway because the Word says you are. And that settles it! The same is true of being a king! God's Word says you are a king, so act like one.

Someone might say, "Yes, we are going to reign with the Lord in heaven!"

Wrong! Romans 5:17 says that we "reign in life." Our domain of rule is here in this life. We don't wait until we die to reign. We reign right here in this life. Besides, why would we need to reign in heaven? The devil is not there, sickness is not there, and poverty is not there.

"Reign" means to rule over. There is nothing in heaven to rule over. It is in this life that we need to rule. We rule the devil, sickness, and poverty in this life. And how do we rule them? Through law! Your mouth makes the law. What you decree is what will be established for you in this life.

Jesus said, "I tell you the truth, whatever you bind on earth will be bound in heaven, and whatever you loose on earth will be loosed in heaven" (Matt. 18:18). The word "bind" means to declare unlawful. The word "loose" means to declare lawful. How do we bind and loose? Through our declarations! We declare with our mouths!

So, how do you predict your future? First, you must choose what you want in life and know that God's Word promises it to you. Then, you meditate on it until you know without a doubt that the promises of God are for you. Finally, you decree it! You speak it as though it were law!

What thing do you need? If you're sick, you need health. If you're confused, you need wisdom. If you're poor, you need money. If you're a sinner, you need salvation. If you're powerless, you need the baptism in the Holy Ghost.

Decide what you need; be convinced that you are going to get it; then, declare with authority that you have it!

Rudder to Your Life

In James 3:7, it says, "All kinds of animals, birds, reptiles and creatures of the sea are being tamed and have been tamed by man." James is taking us back to Genesis where God told man that He gave him dominion, and he was to rule the animals, the birds of the air, and everything that crept upon the earth (Gen. 1:26). God told him to rule the animal kingdom. Yet Adam's dominion extended beyond the animals. God told him to rule everything. That included the devil and demons.

Now in James chapter three, he shows us how mankind's dominion has been limited. Man can make a lion lie down, but cancer can make him lie down. He can make an elephant stand up on one foot, but disease can make him lose his foot. Why? Because there's one area that man can't control—and that's the tongue. "But no man can tame the tongue" (James 3:8). Because of this, man can't rule like God intended him to rule. This is why man can be so defeated in life.

Sickness can destroy him. Poverty can pulverize him. Natural catastrophes can demolish him. He can rule the animals, but he can't rule the elements in the world. James shows that if man can get control of his tongue, he can rule completely and thoroughly:

> *For we all often stumble and fall and offend in many things. And if anyone does not offend in speech* [never says the wrong things], *he is a fully developed character and a perfect man, able to*

> *control his whole body and to curb his*
> *entire nature.* *(James 3:2 AMP)*

Think about this Scripture for a moment. If you never say the wrong things, you are able to control your whole body. But if you say the wrong things, then you are out of control. If you're out of control, then someone else is in control.

What wrong things do we say? Anything that is contrary to the Word of God is the wrong thing to say. However, if you say the right thing—the Word of God—then your whole body is lined up and under your control.

Your body will line up with the words of your mouth. What you say with your mouth, your body will line up to those words. Now you can understand why certain things happen.

You say, "Oh, I think I'm catching a cold." Then quit running after it.

You say, "About this time of the year, I always get the flu." What happens when you speak like this? Your body lines up to your words. What's really sad is that you are proud that you predicted that you were going to get the flu. You say, "You see, I told you so. I told you that I was going to get sick, didn't I?" Your body is simply lining up with your words.

Yet, the Bible says that if you never say the wrong thing, then you're a perfect man, able to keep your body under control. This is dominion. This is control, and you can have it.

Suppose your doctor has given you a negative report: "I'm sorry to inform you that you are going to have this pain for the rest of your life." Let me tell you something. Your body is not meant to be under the control of someone else's words; it's meant to be under the control of your tongue.

You should simply thank him for his diagnosis and then declare, "Jesus bore my sicknesses and carried my diseases in His own body, and with His stripes I am healed!" Don't say, "I guess I better plan to retire." No! Shout the Word of God! As you begin to speak the Word, your body will line up with it.

You might say, "But I'm crippled. I don't have any strength to continue working." Then start speaking the Word that says, "The Lord is the strength of my life!" (Ps. 27:1 KJV).

Healed of Arthritis

There's a lady in my church who just reached the age of forty. She began to feel a sharp pain in her left elbow. The pain eventually traveled throughout most of her arms. She thought, "It is only natural at my age that I should get arthritis." But after hearing the Word, she began pushing those thoughts out of her mind. She refused to verbalize her pain.

Her husband and children knew the pain she was going through because, one day while she was exercising with her daughters, suddenly she couldn't move her arms. She even got to the point that she couldn't do her household chores. Even though her family was very concerned for her, she continued to keep her tongue from speaking arthritis.

One Sunday morning, the Lord gave me a word of knowledge: "The Lord wants to heal a woman who has pain in her arms. This week you have had a lot of pain. Come forward for prayer if that's you."

Immediately, she and her daughters turned to look at each other. She didn't hesitate one moment. She ran forward and was gloriously healed.

Learn something from her example. Don't verbalize your fears; instead verbalize your faith. You may have to confess for forty years that you are strong before you see any difference. But say it anyway. Sooner or later your body has to line up with your words.

This is my declaration: Every organ, every tissue of my body functions in the perfection that God created it to function in. I refuse to allow viruses, infection, or allergies into my body. Anything bad that tries to attack my body instantly dies. My body is the temple of the Holy Spirit; therefore, only good is in my body.

What am I doing? I'm predicting the future of my body. This is what James says the tongue can do.

> *When we put bits into the mouths of horses to make them obey us, we can turn the whole animal. Or take ships as an example. Although they are so large and are driven by strong winds, they are steered by a very small rudder wherever the pilot wants to go. Likewise the tongue is a small part of the body, but it makes great boasts. Consider what a great forest is set on fire by a small spark. The tongue also is a fire, a world of evil among the parts of the body. It corrupts the whole person, sets the whole course of his life on fire, and is itself set on fire by hell.* (James 3:3–6)

I asked the Lord one time, "Why is James so negative about the power of the tongue?

After all, Proverbs 18:21 says that death and life are in the power of the tongue. The tongue can be used for evil and good, but why does James seem to focus on the evil that the tongue produces?"

The Lord answered, "Because James is speaking to the majority of people. Most people are negative; most people use the tongue for evil and not good. The tongue too often is poison instead of the balm of Gilead. Most people are speaking death instead of life, curses instead of blessings."

Let me give you an example. Suppose you come out of a mall with your children, and, as you walk to your car, you see someone kicking the tires of his car and cursing, "You no-good-for-nothing car! I don't know why I bought you! You are a lemon!" Does that incident surprise you? Of course not. In fact, you might think, He probably bought his car from the same dealer that I did.

Now, let's change the situation. You come out of the same mall with your children. You walk to your car and see a man smiling at his car, hugging it, and saying, "Oh, car, I love you. You are so good to me. You never break down. I'm so glad I bought you." What are you thinking? You think that man is crazy. You grab your children and walk away from him.

You think something is wrong with him because he is so positive.

This illustration proves that we are accustomed to negativity. This is why James appears to use the tongue in a negative way, because most people are accustomed to negativity.

Now you don't have to be negative. Your tongue can be used for the good. However, it's up to you.

Setting Your Course

Notice that James uses three analogies to describe the tongue. He describes it as a rudder to a ship, a bit in a horse's mouth, and a small spark. They are all very small, just like the tongue. Out of all the parts of the body, the tongue is one of the smallest parts, yet it is the most powerful part of the body. Your tongue is the most powerful instrument you possess.

A rudder is used to determine the direction of a ship. The wind may be blowing from the west, and normally the ship would be blown off course, but with a rudder the ship can go right into the storm and stay on course.

The same is true of your tongue. The winds of sickness and poverty may be blowing against you, but by the rudder of your tongue you can sail right into the storms of life and go the opposite direction. You don't have to be carried away by the storm. You can use your tongue as a rudder by saying, "Winds of sickness are not going to blow me off course from the Word of God. I'm going right against the storms by declaring that I'm healed by the stripes of Jesus." Your tongue acts as a rudder and keeps you healthy despite the storms of life.

The winds of poverty may blow against you, trying to get you off the course of God's plan for your prosperity. But, you simply maintain your course by saying, "Jeremiah 29:11 says that God has a plan for me, and it is a plan to prosper me. It is a plan to give me hope and a future." You see what you are doing: you are charting your course by the words of your mouth.

Determine Your Destiny

Just as a rudder determines the destiny of a ship, so you are determining the destiny of your life by the words you speak. Your words are predicting your future.

James also says that your tongue is like a bit in the mouth of a horse. A horse may want to go one way, but the bit tells the horse where to go. The rider is in charge, because he controls the bit. You're the rider. You control the direction of the horse. How? Not because you are bigger and stronger than the horse, but because of a little bit. That bit makes the horse obey you.

You see, diseases may be stronger than you, but you can control them by your words. Your words can make cancer shrink. They can make your immune system function correctly. Your words can make your life better, as long as your words line up with God's Word. Let me remind you, you can't simply echo what you hear from others. The Word of God must be personally real to you.

Your tongue also can destroy your life. We know this because James also describes the tongue as a little spark that sets a forest on fire. He says that this little spark "sets the whole course of his life on fire" (v. 6). Your tongue **sets the whole course** of your life. Your course is the future direction of your life. Your tongue determines the future of your life.

You may not be aware of it, but simple little words like these can destroy your life: "Nothing ever works for me"; "I'm always getting sick"; "I'm never going to amount to anything"; "I never have enough money to pay the bills." These words are like little sparks that do not look devastating, but they can set your life on fire from hell. You give hell permission, through your words, to bring these things into your life.

Now listen carefully, you cannot say with your mouth that you are healed and prosperous and then also say that you are sick and poor. When you do that, you have what the Indians call "a forked tongue." You say one thing, then you contradict yourself and say something else. You cannot use your tongue that way and expect positive results. James rebukes this kind of talk:

> *Out of the same mouth come praise and cursing. My brothers, this should not be. Can both fresh water and salt water flow from the same spring? My brothers, can a fig tree bear olives, or a grapevine bear figs? Neither can a salt spring produce fresh water.* (James 3:10–12)

James is saying that if you have both fresh water (that's good) and salt water (that's bad) coming from the spring, then you get salt water. In other words, the fresh water does not overcome the salt water. Salt water will always make fresh water salty. Isn't that right?

The same is true of the tongue. Your negative words will usually cancel out your positive words. The reason is simple: We live in a negative world that has been plunged under a curse. The world is like a stream—and water always flows downward. It takes greater effort to go up the stream.

This is why you can say **many** positive things, then in a moment of doubt say **one** thing that's negative, and you'll end up canceling the positive confession of God's Word. This is why you must guard your tongue. You must pray like David, "I will put a muzzle on my mouth" (Ps. 39:1) so that I don't sin against you.

Of course, we all make mistakes, so don't give up and think that you can never have the good things that God has promised you because you sometimes say things that are not in line with God's Word. But, do try to improve.

It's time that you chart a new course for your life. You do it by speaking words of health, words of prosperity, words of victory, words of success—all the time. And don't let any cursing—saying bad things—come out of your mouth.

You Can Predict Your Future
by saying...

I am a king. I reign in life through Jesus Christ.

I am in charge of my life through God's power. I am not subject to the world's troubles.

I am a priest and a king.

I live by faith, not by sight. It doesn't matter what I feel like; I am a king.

I reign in life through Jesus Christ.

I rule over Satan and his cohorts. I tread on serpents and scorpions. Nothing they try to do can harm me. I am under God's protection.

I have the keys of the kingdom of God. What I bind, heaven binds. What I loose, heaven looses.

I bind all forces of evil in my life. I loose all the blessings of God into my life.

I put a guard over my mouth. I refuse to say anything wrong. I speak only God's Word.

My body lines up to the words of my mouth. What I say is what I get. My body works perfectly, just the way God intended it to work.

I don't verbalize my fears. I verbalize only my faith.

It doesn't matter what trials come my way; I only speak what is a good report. The report of the Lord is I'm healed, I'm blessed, I have the victory through faith in Jesus Christ.

I am raised up with Christ and made to sit with Him in heavenly places. I am on top of the world.

Chapter 8

Words Are Tomorrow in Today

Imagine sitting in an airplane and hearing the pilot's voice, "Hello, this is Captain Lost. Our goal is to arrive somewhere. I don't know where I'm going, but I hope to arrive there anyway." That is your cue to get off the plane.

A pilot has a map that tells him where to go. You have a map that tells you where to go and where God wants you to be. It's called the Bible. The Bible contains thousands of promises for us: from healing to prosperity, to guidance, to victory, to happiness in every realm of life. It is in these promises that you will find your glorious future. Unfortunately, many people do not avail themselves to these glorious promises. Therefore, they don't have a glorious future.

The Power of Words

In the Bible God tells us how this great future can come to pass in our lives. It comes to pass through our words. God has ordained our words to be the rudder of our lives. What we say will determine our destiny. Solomon said:

From the fruit of his lips a man is filled with good things as surely as the work of his hands rewards him. (Prov. 12:14)

Working with your hands will produce certain results for you. Work will determine your future. If you don't work, then you will have a bad future. It's just that simple.

Yet God says that your tongue can produce the same kind of results as the work of your hands. Solomon is saying that a man is filled with good things by the fruit of his lips.

If you had a choice between having good things or bad things, wouldn't you choose the good things? Of course you would. Well, how do you get the good things? By the fruit of your lips.

Let's look at another Scripture which echoes this truth: "From the fruit of his lips a man enjoys good things" (Prov. 13:2). How does a man enjoy good things? By the fruit of his lips. Now let's look at the classic Scripture on the power of the tongue:

> *From the fruit of his mouth a man's stomach is filled; with the harvest from his lips he is satisfied. The tongue has the power of life and death, and those who love it will eat its fruit.*
>
> *(Prov. 18:20–21)*

What you say out of your mouth is going to determine whether you have life or death. Your words determine whether you are going to have blessings or curses.

When the Bible speaks of the tongue, it is not referring to the pink, wet, slimy muscle in your mouth. It is referring to the words that the tongue speaks. Don't be like the woman who said, "I'm always saying the wrong thing. I think it's because my tongue is wet, and it's always slipping." The tongue is a muscle of speech. It is speech that is powerful, not the muscle itself.

This Scripture says that the tongue produces fruit. We could say it this way: your words produce fruit, and fruit is the end result of seeds. If you hold in your hand an apple, then you hold the end result of a seed. So, fruit is the end result of a seed.

This means that your words are initially seeds. What you plant now, you will get later. So, what you say now, you will get later.

My friend, Don Gossett, wrote a best-selling book entitled, *What You Say Is What You Get*. This is true. What you say now, you will get later. You are going to reap the words of your mouth. So, you better watch what you say, because if it is bad you will reap it. This is one of the most powerful truths that you can learn when it comes to successful living.

Promise of Tomorrow

Every seed holds the promise of tomorrow. Tomorrow is the future. Every seed holds the promise of the future. Your words hold the promise of your future. The life you are living now is the result of the words you spoke in the past.

I've heard parents say, "We don't understand why our kids didn't turn out right. We did everything we could. We even warned them. We told them that they were never going to amount to anything. We told them that they were going to be failures…and they were."

Do you see what these parents did? They constantly spoke negative things to their children. They predicted the future of their children by their words.

You say, "Wait a minute. Aren't we supposed to warn our children when they do wrong?" Yes. You can warn them without predicting that they are going to have a bad future, though.

For example, after your son has done something wrong you can spank him and then say, "Son, what you did was wrong. Jesus lives in you, so you can do better. Next time, let the Lord live through you. I forgive you." That's better than saying in anger and fear, "You're never going to amount to anything! I won't be a bit surprised to find you in prison some day!"

I have noticed that nearly every Miss America winner will say something like, "I want to thank my parents for their support. They told me that I could do anything if I put my mind to it. They believed in me and said that I could be Miss America. Thank you, Mom and Dad, for believing in me."

You hardly ever hear any winner say, "I thank only myself because no one believed in me. My parents said that I was foolish in thinking that I could be Miss America." No! You don't hear those lovely ladies say that.

Unfortunately, you may be walking in the fruit of your parents' negative words. Maybe they told you over and over again that you would never amount to anything. Don't believe them. Believe God's report instead.

> *Who is it that overcomes the world? Only he who believes that Jesus is the Son of God.*　　　*(1 John 5:5)*

> *With God all things are possible.*
> 　　　　　　　　　　*(Matt. 19:26)*

> *The one who is in you is greater than the one who is in the world.*　　*(1 John 4:4)*

> *For though a righteous man falls seven times, he rises again.*　　*(Prov. 24:16)*

> *We know that in all things God works for the good of those who love him, who have been called according to his purpose.*　　　　　　*(Rom. 8:28)*

Start speaking God's Word, and don't repeat the negative words of others, even if those people happen to be your parents. Love your parents, respect them, and be kind to them, but don't believe their negative reports about you.

In Numbers chapter fourteen, the people were declaring that they and their children would die in the desert and not enter the Promised Land. God spoke to Moses and told him to give them this message: "As surely as I live, declares the LORD, I will do to you the very things I heard you say" (Num. 14:28). God tells them that they are going to get everything they said. God said to them that what they say is what they get. God did, however, exempt the children: "As for your children that you said would be taken as plunder, I will bring them in to enjoy the land you have rejected" (Num. 14:31). So you see that your parent's words do not have to determine your destiny.

Good and Bad

Proverbs 18:21 says that the tongue can produce both life and death. It can be an instrument of good and of bad. The tongue is neutral. It's neither good nor bad; it's only an instrument. You can use it to produce good or you can use it to produce bad. The choice is yours.

Your tongue even has the power of health. "The tongue that brings healing is a tree of life" (Prov. 15:4). "Reckless words pierce like a sword, but the tongue of the wise brings healing" (Prov. 12:18).

Your tongue can make you well. Doctors have known this for some time. Some patients have told their doctors that they would "live and not die" (Gen. 43:8), and they did. These patients should have died according to the doctor's reports, but instead they lived. Such miracles have constantly baffled the medical profession. I'm convinced that in many of these miracle cases, the people got healed because of their words.

Mary Bustillos is one person who got healed because she maintained a positive confession of God's Word. Mary is one of my deaconesses at church. In 1986, Mary began to experience excruciating pain in her breast. During this time she cried out to Jesus, "Have mercy on me!" At this time, Jesus appeared to her in a bright light and showed her his nail-scarred hands. Mary thought, Oh, my God! I'm going to die because I have seen the Lord. Because of this vision, Mary gave up hope of living, thinking that the Lord was coming to take her to heaven.

She shared this vision with a sister in the Lord who was from Albuquerque. This lady helped Mary understand this vision. She rebuked Mary by showing her that she was misinterpreting the vision: "Jesus is showing you, Mary, that He bore your sickness, not that He is going to take you home." Most importantly, the lady told Mary, "Quit speaking about dying. Speak life and healing." She did, but the symptoms worsened.

Finally, she went to see a doctor about this condition. The doctor gave her the news that every woman has feared hearing, "You have cancer. Unfortunately, it's already in the last stage. We can't do anything to help you."

Despite the negative report from the doctor, Mary began to declare, "The cancer is dead. The tumor is shrinking. I shall live and not die, and declare the glory of the Lord" (see Ps. 118:17). This sounded silly to the doctors, but to their amazement the cancer eventually disappeared. They gave her a complete bill of health in 1988. She is still alive and well and working hard for the Lord.

Mary and others like her have talked themselves into health. Others, unfortunately, have talked themselves into dying. Sometimes there was nothing seriously wrong with them, but they died anyway. Their words killed them.

Your words have the power of life and death. Your words are the most powerful thing you have working for you or against you. So, make your words work for you!

You Can Predict Your Future
by saying...

I have no reason to fear the future. God has plans to prosper me and not harm me. He has plans to give me hope and a future.

I am following God's plan for my life.

I know where I'm going because I have God's wisdom in my life. Jesus has given me wisdom from God.

I am filled with good things by the fruit of my lips.

Life and blessings are on my tongue. I speak only the good and not the bad.

The life I am now living is the result of the words I spoke in the past. So, I am speaking good things now; later my life will become these good words.

I will not walk in the negative words that people have spoken over my life. I bind those negative words from my life.

I can do all things through Christ who strengthens me.

I will live and not die, and I will declare the glory of the Lord.

I am a world overcomer.

Greater is the Holy Spirit who is in me than the devil who is in the world.

All things work together for my good because I love God and am called according to His good purpose.

Chapter 9

The Choice Is Yours

We all want a good future, but simply desiring it will not make it come to pass. Even though a good future doesn't just happen, a bad future will.

Why? Because this world has been plunged under a curse.

After Adam sinned, God told him, "Cursed is the ground because of you...It will produce thorns and thistles for you" (Gen. 3:17, 18). In Texas we call thorns and thistles "tumble weeds". Every year after the Fall, we have had to work hard to produce fruit instead of weeds. Have you ever noticed that you don't have to work hard to produce weeds? Weeds grow automatically.

I have a beautiful, green, lush lawn. When I bought my house, though, there was hardly any grass, because the house had been unoccupied for several months. When I moved in, I plowed the ground, planted seeds, fertilized, and watered. Then, I had to spray weed killer. Now, all I have to do is skip a couple of weeks of watering, and do you know what happens? The grass turns yellow; the weeds start growing; the lawn starts withering. Why? Because we live in a cursed creation.

Your future is like my lawn: if you do nothing about it, then your future will turn bad. Even if you try to change your future in the energy of the flesh, you'll still produce failure. That was the lesson Adam learned. He tried to succeed by "the sweat of [his] brow" (Gen. 3:19). Sweat comes from the flesh. Adam worked and worked according to the manner of the flesh, yet despite his hard work he produced thorns and thistles.

But, praise God! Jesus wore the thorns on His head in order to redeem us from producing thorns, so now we can produce fruit! Jesus redeemed us from the curse so that we can enjoy the blessing. We don't have to produce thorns and thistles any longer.

Making Things Happen

Let me make an important statement to you. **If you are not making things happen,**

then you are letting things happen! If you are waiting for God to change your situation without you doing your part, then you are sorely deceived.

You might be thinking, "Where, then, does God fit into all this?"

It's simple. God has already predicted a wonderful future for you. The Bible calls this predestination. Predestination comes from two words: *pre* which means "before" and the word *destination* which means "the place a person travels to." In other words, God has decreed your destination—your future. Predestination is God's foreordained plan for you.

Predestination is not automatic, though. It doesn't just happen without you doing your part. People have mistakenly associated predestination with fatalism. Fatalism is the doctrine which proclaims that all events are predetermined or subject to fate—something that unavoidably befalls a person.

Many people have the philosophy of Doris Day's famous song, "Que sera, sera; Whatever will be, will be." This song is wrong. Life is not full of chances; it's not ruled by luck.

Your life is going to be determined by what you believe. And if you believe and speak the Bible, then your life will be filled with God's promises.

The Bible teaches that there are reasons why certain things happen in this world. The spiritual realm, to a certain extent, governs this natural realm we live in. Angels protect us while demons try to kill us. (See Ps. 34:7 and James 5:8.) Sometimes, the devil and demons don't need to do anything to us because we destroy ourselves.

I remember counseling a mother and her daughter. The daughter was experiencing grief, because her fiancé was tragically killed in a motorcycle accident. They came to me for answers, wanting to know why this young man had died.

I'm sure they were expecting me, a minister, to give some profound, spiritual reason as to why this man died, such as, "Well, sisters, God's ways are not our ways. The death of this man is a blessing in disguise. One day, you'll understand why!" I can't stand answers like that. Those types of answers are empty religious rhetoric.

So, you might be wondering what I told those two ladies who were wondering why the man died. I answered their question by first asking them, "Was the young man wearing a helmet?"

They answered, "No! But we begged him to wear his helmet. He just wouldn't listen to us."

I said, "I believe I have the answer to why this man died."

"You do?"

"Yes. The reason he died was because...well...because he didn't wear his helmet."

The two women looked shocked. "What do you mean that he died because he wasn't wearing his helmet?"

"Did the doctors say that he would have lived if he wore his helmet?" I asked.

"Yes, but..."

I interrupted, "You see, the doctors agree with me that he died because he refused to put on his helmet." I proceeded to explain to them about human responsibility.

These two sincere ladies had a fatalistic view of God. They thought God had preordained certain things to happen that we couldn't change.

This reminds me of a religious call-in radio program in which a grieving father asked the minister, "I feel so depressed. I lost my little girl to cancer. She was only three years old. Why did the Lord take her?"

I wanted to jump in and shout, "The Lord didn't take her! (God doesn't kill, although He does take a person's soul into heaven once he dies.)

Someone might argue, "But the Lord gives and the Lord takes away" (see Job 1:21). That's not true, at least, not in the sense that many mean it.

"It's in the Bible!" you say.

Yes, it's in the Bible. Job said it, but not in the sense that he believed that God was actually the cause of his problems or that God was to be blamed for his troubles. Remember, also, he spoke from his limited knowledge of God. God holds us accountable for what we know. From everyone who has been given much, much will be demanded. Job spoke the truth according to his knowledge; therefore, he was not blaming God for his troubles like many do today.

"In all this, Job did not sin by charging God with wrongdoing" (Job 1:22). This proves that when Job said, "The LORD gave and the LORD has taken away" (Job 1:21), he was not saying it as an accusation against God, or even, necessarily, believing that God killed his family and made him sick. After all, Job probably understood that Satan stole from him, or else how could the author of Job describe Satan as the one who afflicted Job?

It's possible to say, "The Lord gave and the Lord has taken away," if you are saying it in the sense that you are still committed to serving God and you know that everything you have belongs to God anyway.

Here is another thought: God appeared to Job and asked him, "Who is this that darkens my counsel with words without knowledge?" (Job 38:2). The obvious answer was Job!

Job admitted this. "Surely I spoke of things I did not understand" (Job 42:3). Job acknowledged that many of his words were spoken beyond his understanding at the time.

From the New Testament, though, we discover the truth about the cause of tragedy, especially sickness. Jesus treated diseases as curses. He did not see them as blessings. If He did, then He would have prayed for people to be sick. Instead, He prayed for their healing. Often, He even attributed people's sicknesses to the works of demons.

If you're still not sure concerning the cause of Job's sufferings, then consider this: we're given behind-the-scenes details as to why Job lost his property, family, and health.

Chapters one and two of Job clearly reveal that Satan stole from Job. Job 2:7 says, "So Satan went out from the presence of the Lord and afflicted Job with painful sores from the soles of his feet to the top of his head." Who afflicted Job? Satan did! Don't accuse God of causing tragedy. The Scriptures, especially the

New Testament, unequivocally teach that God brings us good while the devil brings us evil. We'll discuss this later in chapter ten of this book.

Nevertheless, the minister who was hosting the call-in program answered the grieving father with these words: "God took your daughter from you because heaven was lonely without her."

I thought, If that were true—if it was really lonely up there—then I wouldn't want to go to heaven. Can you really picture the saints in heaven saying, "I'm sure getting lonely, God. Please, Lord, give my wife cancer, so she can keep me company up here"? Of course you can't imagine the saints in heaven saying those things.

Bible Predestination

Ministers like this fellow on the radio and Christians everywhere give answers such as this because of their misunderstanding of predestination. Predestination is not hard to understand. This doctrine is only mentioned specifically four times in the New Testament (See Rom. 8 and Eph. 1.)

Every time predestination is mentioned, it refers only to positive things. God predestined us to be adopted into His family. He predestined us to be conformed into Christ's likeness. Nothing is directly mentioned about people being predestined to hell or anything terrible, nor does the Bible use the term predestination to mean that every event in our lives is preordained by God. Yes, God knows everything that will happen in our lives, but He does not cause everything to happen.

The Bible teaches general predestination, that God has preplanned a family; not specific predestination, that God has preordained every event in our lives.

"He predestined us to be adopted as his sons through Jesus Christ" (Eph. 1:5). It was a family that God predestined.

In the beginning, God created Adam to be His son. God had always planned to have a family in His image. He planned this before the creation of the world, so you had nothing to do with it.

"Didn't God choose us to be in His family?" you might ask.

Yes, God chose us according to His foreknowledge. But he planned for the whole world to be saved by making provision for all to be saved. First John 2:2 says, "[Christ] is the atoning sacrifice for our sins, and not only for ours but also for the sins of the whole world." Provision was made for the **whole world** to be saved and adopted into God's family. Those who are not saved have no one to blame but themselves!

Many harp on the fact that God chose us, therefore, implying that we had no part to play in being chosen by God. But, remember that First Peter 1:2 says, "[You] have been chosen according to the foreknowledge of God the Father." Notice the word *according*. In other words, God's election is dependent on His foreknowledge and omniscience. This means that God picked us knowing ahead of time what we would do.

For example, if a gambler knew all things, then he would be able to pick which horse would win the race. But, you wouldn't say that the gambler is the cause of the horse winning or the fault of the other horses losing.

It should be understood that God is not compatible with a gambler. This is simply an analogy to help people understand predestination. I am not trying to bring God down to the level of a gambler anymore than Jesus was trying to bring God down to the level of an "unjust judge" (Luke 18:6) or Himself to the level of a "thief in the night" (Matt. 24:43–44).

This illustration can help us understand God's sovereignty. He knows all things. Therefore, he can pick and choose which person will be in His family, but He is not solely the cause of people coming into His family or the fault of people not coming into His family. Jesus gave us a parable to illustrate this truth:

> *The kingdom of heaven is like a king who prepared a wedding banquet for his son. He sent his servants to those who had been invited to the banquet to tell them to come, but they refused to come....Then he said to his servants, "The wedding banquet is ready, but those I invited did not deserve to come. Go to the street corners and invite to the banquet anyone you find....For many are invited, but few are chosen.*
>
> *(Matt. 22:2–3, 8–9, 14)*

Please answer this: Who was invited to the banquet? **Anyone** who wanted to come!

> *Everyone who calls on the name of the Lord will be saved.*   *(Rom. 10:13)*

> *This is good, and pleases God our Savior, who wants all men to be saved and to come to a knowledge of the truth.*
>
> *(1 Tim. 2:3–4)*

Here is the other question: Who was considered chosen? The few who agreed to come. The people who went to the banquet determined that they were the chosen ones.

The king did not randomly choose who he invited to come to his son's wedding. Rather, he invited anyone who wanted to come, but only those who came became the chosen ones. So you can see that we determine whether or not we become the chosen ones.

You Decide

This day I call heaven and earth as witnesses against you that I have set before you life and death, blessings and curses. Now choose life.   (Deut. 30:19)

Choose life. He did not say, "Since I don't like you, I think I'm going to give you death and curses. But, you, good-looking person, I like you, so I'm going to give you blessings."

You see, we often think that God makes the choices as to whether or not we get blessed. Many think, "Well, if God wants to bless me, He will just bless me. It's up to Him. I hope He blesses me, but it's up to the Lord. Because I'm so humble, I'll accept whatever God has for me." **Wrong**!

God said that He calls "heaven and earth as witnesses against you." He is making sure that every angel in heaven records what He is saying and that every demon in hell notes these words of His! He is making sure everyone understands this one thing—that He has set before mankind life, death, blessings, and curses, and that it is up to each person to decide for himself what he wants—blessings or curses. God is not choosing for him. He must decide for himself, and the life the person gets is a result of the choice he made. Period!

Just in case you're not smart enough to make the right choice, God exclaims, "Now choose life!"

"Oh, Lord, I'm so humble that I'm going to leave the decision with You. In fact, I'm so very humble that I'm going to choose the curses to make me more humble." Now, I'm exaggerating the way people think, but some do come rather close to thinking this way.

If God wanted me to be cursed, then He would not have told me to choose the blessings. He wants me to be blessed. You might say to me, "Well, Tom, what if I don't choose either blessings or curses?" Then, you'll get the curses because, as I wrote earlier, the earth is under a curse.

The same thing applies to salvation. You don't have to actually reject Christ to be lost; you simply need to do nothing. "Whoever does not believe," said Jesus, "stands condemned already" (John 3:18). The human race is **already** condemned. You must choose Christ to escape condemnation. Do nothing, and you "stand condemned." The Bible is clear in its teaching: everyone is born in sin and born under the curse.

Ezekiel saw a multitude in the "valley of decision." Maybe you're in that valley. What if you choose neither left nor right—Satan nor God? Instead, you just stay in the valley. Guess what happens? The valley gets flooded. That's what will happen to you if you don't make a decision.

We all begin life in the valley. Don't stay there. Choose life, choose Christ, and live! Choose to believe His Word and to speak it out of your mouth.

You Can Predict Your Future
by saying...

Jesus bore the thorns to redeem me from the curse. I can produce fruit.

I am a fruit-bearing branch of the vine of Jesus Christ.

In Him I live, move, and have my being. I am a new creature in Christ Jesus.

I am not going to let things happen to me. I am going to make things happen through my authority as a child of God.

My success has nothing to do with luck or chance; it has to do with Jesus. He is my Lord! He is my boss.

I am a new creature in Christ Jesus. The old me has died. The new me is full of joy, peace, and love.

Angels protect me and encamp around me because I trust in the Lord.

God is good and never brings tragedy into my life.

I am blessed with all spiritual blessings in heavenly places in Christ Jesus.

God has predestined me to be conformed into the image of His dear Son.

I am adopted into God's family. I can call God, "Father."

I am one of His chosen ones. He picked me for His family because He wanted to.

God has set before me life and death. So, I choose life.

There is now no condemnation for me because I am in Christ Jesus. I have chosen Christ because He has chosen me!

Chapter 10

Believe for Healing

Job 22:28 says, "What you decide on will be done and light will shine on your ways." The Amplified Bible puts it like this: "...and the light [of God's favor] shall shine upon your ways." God's favor can be upon your future, but the thing that you must do is decide.

Decide on a thing! Decide what you want! "Decide" means to determine and settle a question, controversy, or struggle by giving victory to one side. There are so many questions and controversies that people struggle with in the Bible. You must decide to give victory to one side, especially concerning the Bible's teaching on healing and prosperity.

People often say, "Well, that's just it, I don't know what I believe about healing and prosperity. I hear one preacher say one thing that gives me faith for healing and prosperity; then I hear another preacher say something else that makes me doubt healing and prosperity. I'm just not sure what the truth is." Well, if you are undecided, then you are never going to get the victory.

You have to make up your mind as to what you believe. You must make up your mind to believe the Bible, not tradition and not what others think. In order to make the right decisions and have strong faith for healing and prosperity, you must be totally convinced that healing and prosperity are your covenant rights. You must have a strong Bible-based opinion on healing and prosperity.

You might be wondering why I'm focusing on the two blessings of healing and prosperity. I am doing so because the Bible says, "Beloved, I wish above all things that thou mayest prosper and be in health" (3 John 1:2 KJV). The two greatest human needs are health and prosperity. The two most often causes of death are sickness and poverty. So, it stands to reason that the Lord has provided victory for us over these two enemies. And He has!

In this chapter, I'm going to focus on healing. A strong belief in healing will set you on the right path for it. Faith for healing will help predict your future health. Deciding to believe in healing will cause the light of God's favor to shine on your path for healing.

According to Your Faith

The deciding factor in the course of your future health is your answer to the question, What do you believe about healing? The following shows the importance of being convinced of God's power to heal:

> *The blind men came to* [Jesus], *and he asked them, "Do you believe that I am able to do this?" "Yes, Lord," they replied. Then he touched their eyes and said, "According to your faith will it be done to you."* (Matt. 9:28–29)

Jesus said that they would be healed according to their faith. It is vitally important to have faith. Your faith releases God to work, and your unbelief hinders God from working for you. In fact, Jesus refused to even pray for these men until He was convinced that their faith was present. The key to receiving your healing from God is to have **faith**!

Jesus often said to those he healed, "Your faith has healed you." (See Matt. 8:13; 9:22; 15:28; Mark 5:34; 10:52)

I remember discussing divine healing with Ophelia, a fellow employee who was taught in her church that Jesus does not heal today and that people who lay hands on the sick are fakes. She said to me, "The trouble with you faith teachers is that you claim that people have to have faith if God is going to heal them, but Jesus healed anyone He wanted at anytime, with or without faith."

I knew that she had not really read the Bible much and was just quoting her pastor. I answered, "That's not true. Don't you know that Matthew 13:58 says, 'And [Jesus] did not do many miracles there because of their lack of faith.'?"

Her eyes opened. "It doesn't say that, does it?" she asked. I nodded. She promised to go home and read that Scripture herself.

The next day, she walked quietly to me and said, "Tom, I read that Scripture you quoted, and it does say that Jesus did not heal because the people lacked faith. I've changed my mind."

I hope you are teachable like Ophelia. She learned that lack of faith can stop God's healing power. Well, if doubt could stop God's healing power, then faith releases God's healing power. So what we need is **faith**.

Since faith comes from hearing God's Word (Rom. 10:17), it is important that you understand what the Bible says about divine healing. It is important that you know what the Bible says about healing, not what men teach about it. Many men claim to preach the Gospel, but they don't get gospel results.

The following incident proves that people will have the faith to be healed when the Gospel is preached without compromise.

> *Where they* [Paul and Barnabus] *continued to preach the good news* [the Gospel]. *In Lystra there sat a man crippled in his feet, who was lame from birth and had never walked. He listened to Paul as he was speaking. Paul looked directly at him, saw that he had faith to be healed and called out, "Stand up on your feet!" At that, the man jumped up and began to walk.* (Acts 14:7–10)

What was the man listening to? He was listening to Paul as he preached the Gospel. Notice that the man had **"faith to be healed."** Where did he get the faith to be healed? He got it from Paul as he was preaching the Gospel. Faith comes from hearing the Gospel. Faith for healing comes by hearing the Gospel of healing.

It is obvious that Paul was not preaching a traditional, man-made, gospel message, "Sorry, God does not heal anymore," or "God does heal sometimes, if He wants to, but you never know what God is going to do. He may use this sickness to chastise you. His ways are not our ways."

This man would never have had "faith to be healed" hearing that kind of religious talk. Yet, this is exactly what most people hear about healing. No wonder they don't see the kind of miracles that are seen in the Bible. They experience too much traditional teaching and not enough biblical teaching.

Three Great Truths about Healing

No one can talk me out of having "faith to be healed." The reason is simple: God taught me three great truths in the Bible concerning divine healing. These are simple truths which are easy to understand. They are irrefutable truths that no one has yet been able to argue against. These truths have kept me strong in faith so that I have been walking in almost perfect health since I've learned these wonderful truths. I have communicated these truths to multitudes and have seen tremendous results. The three truths are the following:

1. Jesus healed **everyone** who came to Him in faith. He never refused to heal anyone. He is the same yesterday and today and forever. He never refuses to heal anyone who comes to Him in faith today.

2. Jesus paid for your healing. He bore your sicknesses and diseases on the cross. Since He bore them, you don't have to have them.

3. Sickness is of the devil. Satan is the author of sickness and disease. You have authority over the devil and can rebuke him and cast him out of your life.

Let's look at these three truths closely.

Jesus Still Heals All

It is clear from the Bible that Jesus healed and healed often. Jesus' main ministry consisted of three things.

Jesus went throughout Galilee, teaching in their synagogues, preaching the good news of the kingdom, and healing every disease and sickness among the people.
(Matt. 4:23)

He taught, He preached, and He healed.

Healing was not a side issue with Christ; it was one of the main issues with Him. So the argument that healing is not that important is contradicted by Christ's own emphasis on healing. He constantly healed the sick.

What about today? Does Jesus still heal? Listen to Hebrews 13:8: "Jesus Christ is the same yesterday and today and forever." Jesus still heals. He has not stopped healing. Some people are surprised that Jesus still heals.

A few years ago, I conducted a miracle rally in my home town of El Paso, Texas. During my message, I felt a tingling sensation come into my right hand. As in times past, I knew this was the power of God coming into me for someone's healing, so I asked people on my right side if they had felt any power coming into them. A young woman named Cynthia Stewart raised her hand and affirmed that she was feeling the power of God.

Weeks before, Cynthia had been in a car accident that left her crippled. Doctors doubted that she would ever walk normally again. She was injured so badly that she could not walk without crutches, and even with the crutches it was difficult. When I saw her raise her hand a terrible thought came to me: Oh, no! What if she doesn't get healed? Then a wonderful thought replaced the ugly one: Jesus can do anything—even make this crippled girl walk!

So I called her to come forward. To everyone's amazement and joy, she arose completely healed. She began to walk in full view of all the people. She even walked without a limp.

Our church was so excited about this miracle that we featured it on television. When we did, I received a threat from an anonymous caller: "I am a lawyer representing a church and I wanted to let you know that we are going to expose you as a fraud!"

I asked who he was and which church he was representing. He refused to tell me. So I said, "Sir, I'm not the healer—Jesus is. So I guess you don't believe in Jesus or the Bible."

He said, "I sure do."

"Then why are you so upset that Jesus did such a great miracle? The Bible tells us He did many miracles. It also tells us that He continued to do miracles through the apostles and through other disciples."

"Yes, I believe He did that back then, but He can't do that anymore!"

I simply laughed. "Sir, if you want to try to expose me, then you are very welcome to try. The first thing you'll need to do is meet the woman who was healed." Yet, that man refused to meet her or me. I think he was afraid to find out the truth—that Jesus still heals!

Someone might say, "Yes, I believe Jesus still heals, but He doesn't want to heal everyone."

Well, then listen to the Word of God:

> *Many followed* [Jesus], *and he healed all their sick.*   (Matt. 12:15)

> [Jesus] *drove out the spirits with a word and healed all the sick.*   (Matt. 8:16)

> *The people all tried to touch* [Jesus], *because power was coming from him and healing them all.*   (Luke 6:19)

How many sick people did Jesus heal? All! Not some or most, but all! It is God's will to heal every believer. Nowhere do we find in the Scriptures that Jesus refused to heal anyone who came to Him in faith. He healed everyone who believed without exception!

Someone might object by saying, "Jesus was the only one who was able to heal all. None of the apostles were able to do that."

This is not true. Look at the following incident in Peter's life:

> *People brought the sick into the streets and laid them on beds and mats so that*

at least Peter's shadow might fall on some of them as he passed by. Crowds gathered also from the towns around Jerusalem, bringing their sick and those tormented by evil spirits, and all of them were healed. (Acts 5:15–16)

So we see that healing was possible for all **after** Christ ascended to God's right hand. This story of Peter healing all clearly demonstrates the possibility that everyone can be healed today. The reason for the apparent failure in the church today has nothing to do with a lack of God's willingness to heal, but rather with the church's unbelief regarding divine healing.

The fact that many people question the subject of divine healing by pointing to others who failed to be healed only proves how doubt and unbelief have penetrated the church. People often defend their ideas against the clear teaching of the Scripture by arguing, "I know people who had perfect faith to be healed. Why did they die and not get healed?"

Don't you see what these people are doing by asking that question? They are trying to crush the clear teaching of Scriptures by pointing to the sad experiences of others. However, the only criteria for determining the truth of anything is the Word of God, not the bad experiences of others.

Many suppose that divine healing should exempt one from physical death, but this is not true. No amount of divine healing will prevent the inevitable death (Heb. 9:27). One should not assume, however, that sickness and disease should be the means by which death comes. God's ideal is that we "check out" of our bodies rather than be evicted from them by sickness and disease.

Many who hold to a different view of divine healing should at least have the courage to use only the Scriptures to prove their theology, instead of using the deceased to draw sympathy toward their persuasion. However, they know how sentimental we are and how we like to view the deceased in a much better light than they usually deserve. Knowing this, these doubt-peddlers take advantage of peoples sentimentality in order to drag them toward their view of divine healing. They do this by eulogizing the deceased. They say with tears, "This dear saint of God had such great faith. I suppose if anyone had faith to be healed, it was Brother So–and–So, but you know how sick he was. He never lived one day of his life without sickness. He was always sick...but he loved the Lord and trusted in Him."

Don't be fooled into that kind of sympathetic argument. Simply say, "I thank God that Brother So–and–So is in heaven and is enjoying perfect health now." Then, leave it at that.

I don't claim to have all the answers as to why some fail to be healed, but I do know one thing: this issue was answered by Christ directly, and very few today ever answer this issue the way that Christ did.

On one occasion, the disciples failed to heal a boy who had epilepsy, so Christ healed the boy. Afterwards, the disciples asked the Lord why they were not able to drive out the spirit of infirmity from that child. Notice Christ' answer. He did not say, "My friends, healing is not possible with everyone. Sometimes God wishes for people to remain sick in order for them to be purified through their sicknesses." Yet, this is the common answer given to why the sick do not get well.

Instead, Jesus answered, "Because you have so little faith" (Matt. 17:20). You see, Jesus knew that God's will was for all to be healed. Jesus never accepted defeat. He never resigned Himself to the belief that certain people should stay sick. No, He looked to heal them all.

Jesus accused the disciples of lacking faith which hindered the boy's healing.

Interestingly, Jesus did not blame the young child's lack of faith or the father's lack of faith for the failure of the boy to get well. We should not blame any individual person for not having faith when someone does not get healed. Instead, we should realize that corporately we are all responsible to a certain extent for the lack of healing in the modern church.

Healing Paid For

Not only did Jesus heal everyone while He was on earth, but to ensure our healing for today, He paid for it. "Surely [Jesus] took up our infirmities and carried our sorrows"(Isa. 53:4).

There you have it: Jesus took up your infirmities, sicknesses, and diseases. Since He took them, you don't have to have them. This Scripture should settle the issue of divine healing once and for all. Yet some people are simply stubborn; they want to argue with God and fight for the right to keep their sicknesses.

Some people try to find reasons why this Scripture does not mean what it says. One preacher told me, "This Scripture is speaking about spiritual healing, not physical healing."

I answered, "I don't see the word 'spiritual' in this verse. You are adding to the Bible."

"But it is understood to mean that because of the context," he continued to argue.

I suggested, "Let Matthew tell you what God meant in Isaiah." He agreed to read Matthew.

> *When evening came, many who were demon-possessed were brought to [Jesus], and he drove out the spirits with a word and healed all the sick. This was to fulfill what was spoken through the prophet Isaiah: "He took up our infirmities and carried our diseases."*
>
> *(Matt. 8:16–17)*

I explained, "It is clear from Matthew that he interpreted the words from Isaiah to mean physical healing, since he quoted it in reference to the healing ministry of Christ."

The pastor paused for a moment and then reluctantly conceded the point.

Sickness Is of the Devil

Another good reason for us to have faith for healing is this: sickness is of the devil, and we don't want anything to do with whatever is of the devil.

Many people are taught that God makes people sick. One man who was taught this was John G. Lake. He was told to accept the fact that his wife was going to die. People told him that the Lord made her sick for a reason, even though they didn't know why.

In the midst of this turmoil, Lake picked up his Bible from the mantelpiece and tossed it on the table. His eyes fell on this Scripture:

How God anointed Jesus of Nazareth with the Holy Spirit and power, and how he went around doing good and healing all who were under the power of the devil, because God was with him.
(Acts 10:38)

Like a flash of lightening these words broke through to his heart: God was not the author of sickness and disease. Satan was the oppressor!

With this new-found truth, he laid hands on his wife and rebuked the devil with all the boldness he had. The power of God flowed through his wife, and then she cried out, "Praise God, I'm healed!"

Lake learned what Jesus clearly understood. Jesus knew who the author of sickness and disease was. After healing a woman who was crippled by a spirit, Jesus said, "Should not this woman, a daughter of Abraham, whom Satan has kept bound for eighteen long years, be set free?" (Luke 13:16). Jesus declared that Satan had bound this woman, not God. This is why Jesus was so bold in his dealing with the sick. He always saw Satan behind the sickness.

From these Scriptures and many others, we see that sickness is not caused by God but by Satan. God tells us, "Resist the devil, and he will flee from you" (James 4:7). We do not have to put up with anything that comes from the devil, and that includes sickness.

I remember sitting down with a lady who was in a wheelchair. I was asked by a brother in the Lord to speak to her about God's healing power and, maybe, pray for her. So I agreed.

Before I could get started, she said, "Don't bother to tell me that God can heal me because God was the One who crippled me."

Surprised at such a remark, I asked her, "Do you believe in the Bible?"

She nodded, "Of course I do!"

Then I told her, "Madam, I'm not going to tell you anything, but I do ask that you read this Scripture and then tell me what it means to you."

I let her read the Scripture in Acts 10:38 about Jesus healing all who were oppressed by the devil. When she read that part, she threw the Bible across the table at me and yelled, "So, you think I'm demon possessed, don't you!?"

I never made a single comment on this verse, but she understood what it meant. She understood that this Scripture clearly shows that the devil is the cause of the physical misery in this world. The only thing she misunderstood was that this Scripture was not saying that anyone who is sick is demon-possessed. It says that Satan is like a thief trying to steal health and healing from us.

I don't blame people for being sick, just like I don't blame people for getting robbed. I never thought that this lady was demon-possessed. I simply knew who the thief was, and I tried to show her that it was not God, but the devil. Unfortunately, because of her firmly held tradition, I was not able to help her. Her problem was that she believed the wrong thing.

You hear people say, "It doesn't matter what you believe just as long as you believe something!" Wrong! If you believe the wrong thing, you are going to receive the wrong thing. So, what do you believe? You better believe what the Bible says. If you believe that Jesus still heals and that He wants you well, that He paid the price for your healing, that sickness is of the devil, and that you have authority over him, then you have begun to predict your future health.

You Can Predict Your Future

by saying...

I believe in divine healing.

I receive healing according to my faith.

Jesus heals all my diseases and sicknesses. He is still the same yesterday, today, and forever.

I make Jesus my doctor and best physician.

Surely, Jesus took up my infirmities and carried my sorrows. By His stripes I am healed.

God is not the author of sickness and disease. Satan is the oppressor, and I resist Satan now.

I forbid Satan to put any disease in my body. My body is the temple of the Holy Spirit.

I resist all symptoms. I live by faith not by sight.

I am in this world, but I am not of this world. I am delivered from this present evil world.

A merry heart does good to me like medicine.

The joy of the Lord is my strength.

God's Word is life and health unto all my flesh.

Every part of my body functions perfectly. My eyes work well. My ears work well. My muscles work well. All my organs work well.

The Spirit that raised Christ from the dead is dwelling inside me and is making alive my mortal body.

Jesus paid for my healing, so I'm walking in health.

Chapter 11

God Wants You Rich

Now that we've seen how we can predict a positive future for our health by aligning ourselves with God's Word, let's move to another area of blessing—prosperity!

I thank God that I grew up in a Pentecostal denomination which taught me about divine healing, yet I don't recall being taught about prosperity. In fact, I grew up with a negative concept about prosperity. I looked at rich people as though they were sinners. I thought that poverty was a sign of virtue.

When preachers began coming to our city preaching on prosperity, our pastor warned us to stay away from these ministers. We never considered that the message of prosperity was in the Bible. I did not heed my pastor's warning—I joined one of those "prosperity" churches.

At first, I had a hard time listening to my new prosperity pastor, because he would give us Scriptures on prosperity that I never knew existed in the Bible. Four Scriptures in particular really stood out above the others, at least to me: 2 Corinthians 8:9, Philippians 4:19, Matthew 6:33, and Malachi 3:10. These Scriptures were foreign to me, yet my eyes began to open as I saw the Word of God on this subject. I hope the Lord will use me to open your eyes.

Redeemed from Poverty

Several years ago some Christian brothers who did not believe in prosperity debated me concerning it. Toward the end of the debate, I quoted this verse:

> *For you know the grace of our Lord Jesus Christ, that though he was rich, yet for your sakes he became poor, so that you through his poverty might become rich.* (2 Cor. 8:9)

After mentioning this verse, one of the brothers said, "The Bible does not say that. If there was a Scripture like this in the Bible, I'm sure my pastor would have told us."

I then challenged him to look up this Scripture in his Bible. I proceeded to tell him to study the context of this passage because many Christians, after discovering this verse, will spiritualize it and try to make it mean that Jesus became poor so that we could become rich spiritually. That Scripture was the first seed which started to change this brother. Soon he embraced the message on prosperity. It is vital that you embrace the message of prosperity because, once you do, you'll have the faith to predict your future prosperity by acting on and confessing God's promises.

Second Corinthians 8:9 can be one of the imperishable seeds which God uses to infuse your spirit with faith for finances. The first thing you must notice concerning this Scripture is the context. It is possible to take any verse in the Bible and use it out of its context. So the question is, What is the context of this verse? What was the apostle Paul talking about?

Paul was talking about giving to the poor saints in Jerusalem. He was collecting an offering for them. Thus, the context is money! It was not salvation or anything spiritual. He was simply talking about money. That is the context of this verse.

So how do we interpret this verse? We interpret it in the light of its context—money. If Paul was talking about salvation, then we would interpret the word *rich* to mean "spiritual" riches. But since he was talking about money, we must interpret it in the light of money.

With that understanding, we come to the main truth: God included prosperity in the plan of redemption. It is clear that Paul is referring to the substitutionary sacrifice of Christ on the cross, because he uses the same terminology earlier in this letter. "God made him who had no sin to be sin for us, so that in him we might become the righteousness of God" (2 Cor. 5:21).

Compare this phrase with the phrase in 2 Corinthians 8:9, and you'll see the similarity. This means that prosperity was included in the work on the cross, which places prosperity as an important aspect of redemption.

Jesus was poor on the cross because He was taking on the poverty that was due to us because of our sins. Sin produces poverty, and He was taking the curse of sin.

Christ redeemed us from the curse of the law by becoming a curse for us, for it is

*written: "Cursed is everyone who is
hung on a tree." He redeemed us in order that the blessing given to Abraham
might come to the Gentiles through Jesus Christ, so that by faith we might receive the promise of the Spirit.*

(Gal. 3:13–14)

Christ was made a curse on the tree, or in
other words "a curse on the cross." This Scripture shows that Jesus took the curse of the law
upon Himself when He was on the cross. What
is the curse of the law? A curse is a
"pronouncement of judgment." This pronouncement is mentioned in Deuteronomy
chapter twenty-seven. There you find God
telling the Levites to pronounce a curse on Israel if they don't keep the commandments of
God.

The curse was shouted on top of Mount
Ebal. In this curse, God pronounced many
"curses" that would come on the people if they
did not obey Him. These curses ranged from
sickness to poverty.

Now, understand what the ramifications
are for us. Since Christ redeemed us from the
curse—the pronouncement of judgment—then
the curses do not belong to us either. So, we
can say that God has redeemed us from the

curses of the law. One of these curses is poverty. The Bible says:

> *All these curses will come upon you. They will pursue you and overtake you until you are destroyed, because you did not obey the LORD your God and observe the commands and decrees he gave you. They will be a sign and wonder to you and your descendants forever. Because you did not serve the LORD your God joyfully and gladly in the time of prosperity, therefore in hunger and thirst, in nakedness and dire poverty, you will serve the enemies the LORD sends against you.* (Deut. 28:45–48)

Notice clearly the description of the curses: hunger, thirst, nakedness, and dire poverty. Now, if Christ took on these curses, you would find Him hungry, thirsty, and naked on the cross. After reading the Bible, you will readily see that Christ was indeed hungry, thirsty, and naked.

From the cross Jesus cried out, "I am thirsty" (John 19:28). Concerning being naked, the Bible says that the soldiers stripped Him of all his clothes and gambled for His clothing. Jesus did not have a stitch of clothing on. He was totally naked! He fulfilled the words in Deuteronomy 28:48 to the very letter.

Why did Jesus become poor? Paul says, "so that you through his poverty might become rich" (2 Cor. 8:9). Praise God! Do you see it? Jesus took the curse of poverty, so that you can take the blessings of Abraham. You can now be rich!

Becoming Rich

First of all, we better define what it means to be rich as a prosperous Christian. Rich means to be abundantly supplied. It means to have the power of God to meet any need. Rich does not mean greedy or extravagant or materialistic. Unfortunately, people associate rich with worldly terminology. Being rich means that Jesus will meet any need, including spiritual, physical, and material needs. Complete prosperity is having all your needs met, not just some.

It does not matter how healthy and rich someone may be; if he has not been saved, then he is poor. Jesus first comes to meet our spiritual needs, and He does this by forgiving us of our sins. He then meets our physical needs. As we have seen in the previous chapter, Jesus constantly healed the sick. You see, someone could have a million dollars and be dying of an incurable disease, and at that point the million dollars means nothing. That rich man is actually poorer than the homeless man who has his health.

On the other hand, a healthy man who's saved and yet is homeless and starving is not very rich either. A rich man is one who is saved, healthy, and has all his material needs met. So, the third need God meets is material.

Many Christians have trouble with believing that they should be blessed with material things, often because of guilt, sometimes because of the world's emphasis on wealth. However, we should accept God's Word concerning God's desire to bless us, even materially.

Meet All Your Needs

The following Scripture was the second verse that helped me to see that God was interested in blessing me, even financially.

> *And my God will meet all your needs according to his glorious riches in Christ Jesus.* (Phil. 4:19)

God doesn't just promise to meet some needs, but He promises to meet **all** your needs. This passage, actually, is dealing more with materialistic needs than spiritual ones. No longer should you accept just having some of your needs met, you should believe that all of your needs will be met, including your house payment, car payment, food, clothes, and everything else.

Seek First His Kingdom

The third truth that changed my life was the following Scripture:

> *But seek first his kingdom and his righteousness, and all these things* [clothes, houses, food] *will be given to you as well.*   (Matt. 6:33)

Contrary to popular opinion, Jesus does want to give us material gifts, but the important thing that Jesus is saying to us is that we must not seek those things. We should only seek God's kingdom and His righteousness; we must focus on His will for our lives. As a result of taking care of God's business, He will take care of our business.

We must delight ourselves in the Lord, and he will give us the desires of our hearts (Ps. 37:4). We can expect to have our desires met as long as our first desire is to please God. This truth must be engrafted into all of our hearts so that we don't go following after money and lose sight of God.

When we lose sight of God, our hearts condemn us, and we don't have confidence that God will meet our needs (1 John 3:20–22). We can confess all day long that God is meeting our needs, but if we are not putting God's kingdom first in our lives, then we are not going to reap the fruit of our lips.

Tithing

The fourth truth about prosperity involves giving. Jesus says, "Give, and it will be given to you." (Luke 6:38). Jesus clearly taught the law of reciprocity: what you give will be given back to you. Not only is this a law, but God also challenges us to test this law:

> *"Bring the whole tithe into the store-house, that there may be food in my house. Test me in this," says the LORD Almighty, "and see if I will not throw*

> *open the floodgates of heaven and pour*
> *out so much blessing that you will not*
> *have room enough for it."*   *(Mal. 3:10)*

Can you hear God's challenge? He is saying, come on, children, test Me by giving your tithes, and I'll show you how many blessings I can pour out on you.

Someone may challenge this Scripture on the grounds that this is the Old Testament. They say, "Tithing is not part of the New Testament. The law of tithing has changed." What's funny about this Scripture in Malachi is that God prefaced what He said about tithing with these words: "I the LORD do not change" (Mal. 3:6). Yet some still declare that God changed this law, despite the fact that God said He doesn't change.

Jesus also clearly proved that tithing is still part of the New Testament. He said,

> *You give a tenth of your spices—mint,*
> *dill and cummin. But you have ne-*
> *glected the more important matters of*
> *the law—justice, mercy and faithfulness.*
> *You should have practiced the latter,*
> *without neglecting the former.*
>
> *(Matt. 23:23)*

Jesus told us not to neglect tithing. His words are the final authority on this subject.

People who still expect to be blessed without tithing remind me of a certain ship captain. He was sailing his battleship through dense fog. Ahead of him, he saw a light which appeared to be coming towards him. He flashed his light in Morse code, "Please, change direction."

The light flashed back, "Sorry, you change direction."

The captain, a little agitated, answered back, "I am a captain. You change direction."

"I am a second class seaman; you change direction, sir."

Furious, the captain flashed back one more time, "I am in a battleship. You change direction!"

The little light flashed back, "I am in a light house—your call."

Many scream in fury, "I don't have to tithe. After all, I'm a child of God. I'm in Christ. God will meet my needs."

When all of that ridiculous screaming is done, God flashes back His answer, "Bring the tithe. After all, I'm God; I'm not moving. I change not. Your call."

There are many more Scriptures that promise prosperity, but the important thing is to find them, meditate on them, meet the conditions that God has commanded, and let them become a revelation to you. Once you do, you'll be ready to confess them boldly and without apology and guilt.

You Can Predict Your Future
by saying...

I know the grace of my Lord Jesus Christ. Though He was rich, yet for my sake He became poor so that I could become rich.

I am rich. I am abundantly supplied. I am highly effective. I am a success in every way.

I use the power of God to meet any need. I do not lack any good thing.

I am a seed of Abraham, so I am blessed along with him. I have his blessings. I walk in the blessings of Abraham.

I remember the Lord, for it is He who gives me the ability to create wealth.

I am blessed so that I can be a blessing.

I refuse to allow the spirit of greed to control my life.

I am a tither and giver. I give, and it is given back to me in good measure, pressed down, shaken together, and running over.

The Lord opens up the windows of heaven and pours out on me so many blessings that I have to yell, "That's enough!"

The devil is rebuked from touching my finances.

Christ has redeemed me from the curse of poverty, so I refuse to be poor.

Poverty is underneath my feet.

I am the head and not the tail. I lend unto many, but I do not have to borrow.

Chapter 12

Why Job Suffered

We have seen from God's Word that healing and prosperity belong to us as children of God and that we should believe and confess the Word for healing and prosperity. Often, when I speak on healing and prosperity, people will ask me about Job. They'll question me, "If healing and prosperity belong to us, why did Job suffer sickness and poverty?" That is a good question, and it deserves to be answered.

First of all, the book of Job was written as a play. Nevertheless, this is not a work of fiction: Job really did exist. Ezekiel 14:14 lists Job as a real, righteous man who once lived long ago. In this play called Job, we find eight characters: God, Satan, Job, Job's wife, Job's three friends (Eliphaz, Bildad, and Zophar), and a young man named Elihu.

The play begins with the narrator telling the story about Job and describing him as the greatest man among all the people of the East. His integrity was world-renowned. He was so upright in the way he lived that even God bragged about him. God told Satan to take note of Job's outstanding life:

> *Then the LORD said to Satan, "Have you considered my servant Job? There is no one on earth like him; he is blameless and upright, a man who fears God and shuns evil."*   *(Job 1:8)*

Satan was disgusted with Job's lifestyle of holiness, so he told God that the only reason Job lived right and worshipped God was because he was so healthy and prosperous. Satan believed that if Job were sick and poor he would quit serving God. So God was going to prove to Satan that Job would serve Him no matter what kind of trials he went through. From there, Satan destroyed everything that Job had—his wealth, his children, and his health.

It is this fact that God allows Satan to destroy everything, which causes all the controversy. Why did God do that?

Well, some charismatics simply blame Job's fears as being the open door to Job's trials. They point to Job 3:25, "What I feared has come upon me; what I dreaded has happened to me." "You see," some exclaim, "Job was operating in fear. This is why Satan was able to attack him."

It is true that fear can cause a lot of bad things to happen to us, but it is also clear that the book of Job is not teaching about fear. You cannot simply take one statement from Job and build an entire theory on it, saying that Job lost it all because of fear. I believe that this interpretation is an over-simplified attempt to explain Job's suffering.

On the other hand, many evangelicals love this story because it proves to them that good men should expect to suffer. The trouble with their view is they forget to point out that Job was healed and blessed twice as much after his trial. In other words, Job did not stay sick or broke. He was healed and blessed.

James reminds us to consider the latter end of Job's life: "You have heard of Job's perseverance and have seen what the Lord finally brought about. The Lord is full of compassion and mercy" (James 5:11).

Isn't it amazing that when people think of Job they think of his trials and not the end of his trials? Yet, James tells us to consider the victory that Job experienced and to let him be an example for us. So, if we are suffering sickness or poverty, we should persevere in faith and God will bring about victory for us, too.

However, that still doesn't answer why God allowed Job to suffer in the first place.

Why Bad Things Happen to Good People

Some think that the book of Job is trying to answer the age-old question, Why do bad things happen to good people? Well, the answer is simple if you don't believe in God. You simply say that life is full of chances. Without God, you don't have to answer the question. But, for people who believe in God, the question is even harder: If God is love and has all the power to remove suffering, why does He allow good people to suffer? Tough question, isn't it? In fact, not only is it tough to answer, it is **impossible** to answer.

What do I mean? Simple. It is possible to ask a question that can't be answered. I do it by asking a question with assumptions. An assumption is something that most people think is true but has not yet been proven. In other words, if I assume something is true, then I cannot ask for an answer to a question unless I am willing to forgo my assumption.

For example, a wife can ask a question with an assumption by saying, "I don't understand how my husband can be a good Christian and yet commit adultery?" Well, he can't be a good Christian and commit adultery. He can be a Christian and commit adultery, but he cannot be a good Christian and commit adultery. Do you see that a person can ask a question that can't be answered?

The same is true of asking the question, "How can God be love and have all power and yet still allow good people to suffer?" This question has three assumptions to it: God is love, God has all power, and good people suffer.

To assume something is not necessarily wrong. In this case, are any of these three assumptions wrong?

First of all, is God love? Of course He is. The Bible says so. "God is love" (1 John 4:16).

Well, how about God's power. Does God have the power to remove suffering?

It is this second assumption that caused a rabbi to write a best-selling book on suffering. Basically, he said that God is love but is not willing to use His power for us. He prefers to let us live our own lives without His intruding upon us. He sees God as a little boy who winds up a toy and then lets it go. He believes God made us and then left us on our own.

But this is not what the Bible teaches in either the Old Testament or the New Testament. Christians rightly refuse to believe that God does not become active in our lives. In the Old Testament we find that God helped Israel out of slavery and delivered Judah from its enemies, and in the New Testament we find Jesus healing the sick and helping the poor. God is active in helping us.

So, the second assumption is correct. God has all the power to help us. "For nothing is impossible with God" (Luke 1:37).

That brings us to the third assumption, "Do good people suffer?"

Job's three friends thought, "No!" They believed that if a person suffered it was because he or she had sinned against God. So throughout the book of Job, they constantly try to get Job to confess his hidden sin. They were very eloquent and knowledgeable, but they were also faultfinders.

Every time they tried to say something to convince Job that he had sinned, Job would claim innocence. Job knew that his troubles did not come because he had committed a sin. He knew that he was not at fault. He didn't understand why God was punishing him since he had not committed any sin.

Although Job's friends were wrong in blaming Job, their words are still considered inspired and should be treated as the Word of God just as Paul does when he quotes one of Job's friends, Eliphaz, in 1 Corinthians 3:19.

It is clear from the first chapter that Job had not done anything bad; in fact, the opposite is true. He was more righteous than anyone, including his friends. He was suffering not because he had done anything bad, but because he was the best man in all of the East. God was putting Job on display.

However, Job's friends did not know this. Instead of seeing Job as being the most righteous man among them, they saw him as the greatest sinner. How wrong they were! If only they had known the beginning of the book, they would have kept quiet.

Because Job was so righteous among men and yet he suffered, people assume that good people suffer. In answering the question, Do good people suffer? you might answer, "Yes, of course they do. Job is the prime example. He was a good person, yet he suffered." So, people think that the book of Job answers yes to the question, Do good people suffer? But if the answer is yes, then God could no longer be just. How can God allow good people to suffer and still be just? He can't.

"Wait a minute! Are you saying that Job was not a good person?" you might ask.

Let me ask you, "Was Job a good person?" Yes? Maybe? Are you sure? Job was not "good" in the sense that the Bible describes what is good.

A rich young man came to Jesus and said, "Good teacher." Jesus interrupted and said that there is no one good but God alone. (See Mark 10:17–18.)

Paul writes,

There is no one righteous, not even one; there is no one who understands, no one who seeks God. All have turned away, they have together become worthless; there is no one who does good, not even one. (Rom. 3:10–12)

The New Testament makes it abundantly clear that no one is considered righteous in God's sight. Now, in man's sight, there are good people. Job was one of them.

The Bible says that Job was the best man in all of the East. That doesn't mean that he was righteous and good in God's sight. He was simply the best man from a human perspective, but even the best man is a sinner in God's sight, and that includes Job. A sinner has no right-standing or rights with God.

Why Job Suffered

The Unforgotten Hero

Do you remember the last character in the book of Job? Elihu is his name. He was not one of Job's friends. He was simply listening to Job's friends judging Job and Job defending himself. As he began to listen to all four, God gave him insight into the true nature of Job's sufferings.

Out of all the human characters, only Elihu understood why Job suffered. It is amazing that I haven't heard anyone ever mention Elihu. We almost forget him. But the truth is, Elihu was the only one with true insight, not only into the sufferings of Job, but insight into the sufferings of all mankind. This is why Elihu is the last to speak concerning Job's sufferings.

It is interesting to note that when God appeared to Job, He rebuked Job for not having insight, and He rebuked Job's three friends for falsely judging Job. Yet God never rebuked Elihu. Why? Because Elihu was correct in understanding suffering.

Elihu begins by saying,

I am young in years, and you are old; that is why I was fearful, not daring to tell you what I know. I thought, "Age

*should speak, advanced years should
teach wisdom." But it is the spirit in a
man, the breath of the Almighty, that
gives him understanding.   (Job 32:6–8)*

Notice, Elihu is about to give wisdom, not
because of any human understanding, but because God's Spirit gave him understanding.
The first thing he does is correct Job's friends.

I waited while you [Job's three friends]
*spoke, I listened to your reasoning; while
you were searching for words, I gave you
my full attention. But not one of you has
proved Job wrong; none of you has answered his argument.   (Job 32:11–12)*

Elihu showed Job's friends that they were
wrong in judging him. The second thing Elihu
does is correct Job, but he does it in humility.

*But now, Job, listen to my words; pay at-
tention to everything I say. I am about to
open my mouth; my words are on the tip
of my tongue. My words come from an
upright heart; my lips sincerely speak
what I know. The Spirit of God has
made me; the breath of the Almighty
gives me life. Answer me then, if you*

*can; prepare yourself and confront me. I
am just like you before God; I too have
been taken from clay. No fear of me
should alarm you, nor should my hand
be heavy upon you. But you have said in
my hearing—I heard the very words—"I
am pure and without sin; I am clean
and free from guilt."* (Job 33:1–9)

Elihu saw one fundamental flaw in Job:
Job believed that he was without original sin.
Job was self-righteous. Yes, he was righteous
as far as men are concerned, but he was not
righteous as far as God was concerned.

Since Job thought he was sinless and not
under the curse of sin, he could not figure out
how he could suffer. This bothered him. But,
Elihu pointed out the fact that Job was a sinner like everyone else and was subject to the
curse of sin which includes sickness and poverty.

People erroneously think that the book of
Job was written to try to answer the question,
Why does God allow good people to suffer? But,
Elihu has no trouble with that question
because he knows that there are no truly
"good" people in God's sight. The thing that
perplexed Elihu was not the fact that Job was
suffering, but the fact that Job's friends

weren't suffering along with Job. In fact, Elihu was wondering why everyone doesn't suffer all the time since everyone is a sinner.

Elihu realized that sinners are under the curse of sin and therefore have no legal right to get mad when they suffer. They should realize that they deserve to suffer, and if they are not suffering, they should praise God even more because He is having mercy on them.

Why Are Sinners Blessed?

Elihu asked the right question, "Why does God allow sinners to be blessed?" The answer: because God is merciful.

In other words, before Job had his trials, he experienced the mercy of God. But, when Job had his trials, he experienced the justice of God; he only got what he deserved.

Immediately after Elihu spoke, God answered Job in a whirlwind and rebuked him for falsely accusing God of injustice. Job wisely repented.

You might be saying, "I understand what you are saying, but how can we claim our healing and prosperity if we are sinners? Sinners, after all, have no right to healing and prosperity."

That was true, before the Cross! But, through the Cross, we have been given the righteousness of God; therefore, we have right-standing with God. We are living after the Cross. This is why God commanded Job's three friends to offer a sacrifice.

God appeared to Eliphaz, the leader of Job's friends, and told him that He was angry with the three of them. He told them that they should take seven bulls and seven rams and go to Job and sacrifice a burnt offering. God said that, when Job prayed for them, He would show mercy on them all and not bring on any tragedy like that which Job experienced. God showed Job and his three friends that only through the shedding of blood is there forgiveness of sins (Heb. 9:22).

This is the point: before Jesus died on the cross for our sins, mankind had no legal right to healing and prosperity. We could only plead for mercy. But now, since Christ has died for our sins, sicknesses and poverty, we have a right to the grace of God.

Difference between Grace and Mercy

Grace is unmerited favor. We do not claim healing and prosperity based on our good works, but based on Christ's good work on the cross.

Remember the Scripture in the previous chapter of this book, "For you know the grace of our Lord Jesus Christ, that though he was rich, yet for your sakes he became poor" (2 Cor. 8:9). He became poor through His substitutionary sacrifice on the cross. Because of it, we have access into God's grace which is far better than mercy.

The Bible tells us to grow in the grace of God. Nowhere does the Bible say to grow in the mercy of God. Many people interchange the word "grace" with "mercy." They think that these two are the same, but they definitely are not.

"Let us then approach the throne of grace with confidence, so that we may receive mercy and find grace to help us in our time of need" (Heb. 4:16). Notice that God's throne is the throne of grace, not mercy. Yet at His throne people can receive both mercy and grace. These are two different things. Unfortunately, most people are trying to receive mercy when they should be finding grace. Grace is better.

What's the difference between mercy and grace? Mercy is when God does not bring on you the punishment you deserve. Grace is when God brings on you the benefits that He paid for. The only similarity between grace and mercy is that both have to do with unmerited favor. However, mercy is not based on legal rights. Grace is!

Let me illustrate the difference. Suppose you are eating a nice meal at a restaurant. Afterwards, you go to the cash register to pay for it. When you reach into your pocket, you discover that you forgot to bring your wallet. You don't have cash, checks, or credit cards. You apologize to the manager and explain that you don't have the money to pay for it. What do you need? **Mercy**! Let's suppose the manager has compassion on you and tells you to forget the bill. You enjoyed the meal without paying for it. This illustrates mercy.

What is grace? Grace is when someone gives you a gift certificate which entitles you to a free meal. So you go to the restaurant and order your favorite food, and you enjoy every bite of it. After the meal, you walk over to the cash register and hand the worker your gift certificate. Do you know what you experienced? **Grace**.

In both cases, you did not pay for the meal. Each time it was unearned favor. In the first case, fear gripped you because you knew you didn't have the money. You were not sure what the manager was going to do to you. There was not an assurance or a peace until you were forgiven, but even then you still felt unworthy because the meal was never paid for.

You see, this is how the Old Testament saints, including Job, operated. They pleaded for mercy but were never sure if God would show it. This is why Job said that he was fearful of tragedy (Job 3:25). He was not confident that blessings would abound in his life all the time because he operated unconsciously by mercy.

In the second case, you enjoyed the meal knowing that someone else paid for it. As long as you had the gift certificate, you ate in peace and confidence. It didn't bother you that someone else paid for it.

You did not walk to the worker at the cash register and say, "Oh, I'm so unworthy to have eaten this delicious meal. I am undeserving of it. Someone else paid for it and gave me this certificate. Do you suppose that you could accept this certificate on my behalf?" No! No! No! A thousand times, no! You went to the register without feeling inferior because you knew that the meal was paid for.

Friend, this is what the New Testament teaches about grace. The gift certificate is the Bible which tells you everything that you are entitled to because of grace. God has already paid the price for your sins, sicknesses, and poverty. You simply come boldly to His throne to find grace in your time of need. You already know that the price has been paid.

You simply present the gift certificate, the Bible, to God and boldly proclaim it. It then becomes yours by faith.

You Can Predict Your Future
by saying...

I live under a better covenant, a covenant that has been ratified by the blood of Jesus.

Jesus is the Guarantee of all the promises of God. He makes sure that I enjoy all my privileges and rights under the new agreement.

I am the righteousness of God in Christ Jesus.

I am growing in the grace of God. I am experiencing God's unmerited favor. I have favor with God and with men.

People look upon me with kindness because I see people as my friends, not as enemies.

I approach the throne of grace with boldness. I have a right to the presence of God.

I receive grace every time I ask for it. I ask, and I receive.

I am as bold as a lion. I refuse to fear anything. I do not fear even when I hear bad news. My heart is fixed on trusting in the Lord.

Wealth and riches are in my house.

My faith may be tested, but I will pass the test.

I inherit all the promises of God through faith and patience.

I will not become bitter toward anyone, even if they slander me. I will pray for those who persecute me.

I'm not afraid of the devil or his schemes. I have dominion over him.

I fear not because for God has not given me a spirit of fear, but of love, power, and a sound mind.

Chapter 13

Determine the Destiny
of Obstacles

Does the good life sound easy? Well, it's not! There are obstacles to the good life.

The Bible says, "Many *are* the afflictions of the righteous" (Ps. 34:19 KJV). This is part of the truth. The other half of this Scripture is, "But the LORD delivereth him out of them all." Many get their minds on the bad part—afflictions—and forget to remember the good part—deliverance!

Jesus says, "In the world ye shall have tribulation" (John 16:33 KJV). I hear people add, "You see, Jesus does not promise us health and prosperity like faith preachers proclaim! He promises tribulation!"

It is true, Jesus does say that we are going to have tribulation. But He doesn't stop there.

He goes on to say, "But be of good cheer; I have overcome the world!" (v. 33). Do you see what Jesus is saying? He says the good life does not come easy. There will be difficulties that you will encounter, but remember that you already have the victory.

Some folks accuse faith ministers of preaching, "Easy victory, no problems, no obstacles, and no difficulties. Just believe and everything will come easily."

I have listened to some of the finest faith ministers of the world, and I have yet to hear one of them say that the faith life is easy. I have not heard one say, "If you have faith, you will never have any more problems and trials." No one preaches that. What people do preach is that you can overcome all the trials of life. Jesus taught that we can determine the destiny of obstacles:

> *The next day as they were leaving Bethany, Jesus was hungry. Seeing in the distance a fig tree in leaf, he went to find out if it had any fruit. When he reached it, he found nothing but leaves, because it was not the season for figs. Then he said to the tree, "May no one ever eat fruit from you again." And his disciples heard him say it...In the morning, as*

they went along, they saw the fig tree
withered from the roots. Peter remem-
bered and said to Jesus, "Rabbi, look!
The fig tree you cursed has withered!"
"Have faith in God," Jesus answered. "I
tell you the truth, if anyone says to this
mountain, 'Go, throw yourself into the
sea,' and does not doubt in his heart but
believes that what he says will happen, it
will be done for him."

(Mark 11:12–14, 20–23)

Jesus determined the destiny of the fig
tree. He predicted its future.

Someone might say, "Yeah, but that was
Jesus. Only He can predict the future." Wrong.

Not only did Jesus show that He could
predict the future of a fig tree, but, more importantly, He told his disciples that they could
do even more by predicting the future of
mountains. Mountains are obstacles.

Jesus is teaching that we can predict the
future of trials. We can determine the destiny
of obstacles. He is saying that faith can predict
the future.

You Move the Mountains

I heard a minister interpret Jesus' lesson
on mountain-moving faith in this way: "Jesus

told you to ask God to move the mountains for you." I almost fell over when I heard this statement.

Didn't this minister ever read the Bible? I thought. Jesus did not say for you to ask God to move the mountains for you. He told you to speak to the mountains yourself. Jesus said, "It will obey you!" (Luke 17:6).

The mountain is not going to just obey **God**. It is going to obey **you**. Don't misunderstand me, God's power is involved in moving the mountains, but the point is, God's power must be released through your spoken word. You must speak God's Word to the mountain in order for the mountain to move. Don't wait for God to speak to the mountain for you. He has commanded you to speak to the mountain yourself.

Of course, God must lead you to move the mountain. You can't simply move whatever mountain you don't like. You must move only those mountains which God wants moved.

At the same time, God is not going to move the mountain without you. This was the error that the minister had made. He interpreted this passage that way because Jesus said, "Have faith in God" (Mark 11:22). He assumed that faith in God means to ask God to take care of something, while you simply watch God do all the work.

Another translation from the original Greek can be found in Alfred Marshall's *The Interlinear Greek-English New Testament* which translates Mark 11:22 as, "Have [the] faith of God" (brackets in the original).[1] There is a subtle yet important difference between having faith **in** God and having the faith **of** God. You'll never move mountains by simply having faith in God. Many people have faith in God and are still not seeing the power of God in their lives. Circumstances are changed only when we use the faith **of** God.

If you're born again, God has deposited within your spirit His very own faith. You have God's faith!

The Faith of God

Critics of the faith message have written scathing books in which they unfairly criticize those who preach that believers have God's faith. In summary, they write that believers could not have God's faith since God does not have faith. As I have read these books, I have thought, If God doesn't have faith, then He must have doubt. If you don't have the positive, you must have the negative.

---

[1] Alfred Marshall, *The NIV Interlinear Greek-English New Testament* (Grand Rapids: Zondervan, 1976), 190.

Of course God has faith! It's terrible to accuse God of not having faith.

The Bible unmistakably teaches that believers have the faith of God available to them. Paul writes in Ephesians 6:11, "Put on the full armor of God." Whose armor are we to put on? God's armor! It is not called "Christian armor"; it's called the "armor of God" for Christians. The pieces of armor are God's fighting clothes. Paul then lists for us the pieces of this armor: truth, righteousness, the gospel of peace, salvation, the Word of God, and **faith**. Faith is part of God's armor; it is a piece of His suit.

In Romans 13:14 Paul says it another way: "Rather, clothe yourselves with the Lord Jesus Christ." This armor is the character of Christ, who is God. Faith is one of God's characteristics which the believer is told to have.

In another place Paul enumerates the characteristics of God which the believer should possess. He writes, "But the fruit of the Spirit is love, joy, peace...faith" (Gal. 5:22 KJV).[2] Notice that faith is one of the fruits of

---

[2] The NIV translates the word *pistis* in this verse as "faithfulness." It should be noted that the NIV usually translates *pistis* as "faith." Many translations, including the King James Version, properly translate this word as "faith."

the Spirit, and the Spirit is, of course, God. The faith Paul mentions is none other than the faith of God!

For example, the other fruits that the believer should bear are "love, joy, peace..." The love we should have is the "love of God [which] is shed abroad in our hearts" (Rom. 5:5 KJV). The peace we should possess is "the peace of God, which transcends all understanding" (Phil. 4:7). And the joy we should experience is the "joy of the LORD [which] is your strength" (Neh. 8:10). Consequently, the faith we should have is the faith of God which "moves mountains" (Job 9:5).

I've given you two Scriptures which prove that the believer has God's faith. "A matter must be established by the testimony of two or three witnesses" (Deut. 19:15). Let me give you one more witness that will establish the matter of the believer possessing a godlike faith.

Through these he [God] has given us his very great and precious promises, so that through them you may participate in the divine nature and escape the corruption in the world caused by evil desires. For this very reason, make every effort to add to your faith goodness; and to goodness, knowledge; and to knowledge, self-control; and to self-control, perseverance;

and to perseverance, godliness; and to godliness, brotherly kindness; and to brotherly kindness, [agape] love. For if you possess these qualities in increasing measure, they will keep you from being ineffective and unproductive.

(2 Pet. 1:4–8)

What are these qualities that we should possess? The qualities of the "divine nature," of course! Notice that Peter includes faith as a part of the divine nature. Peter begins the list of the divine nature with "faith" and ends the list with the highest divine quality of all, "[agape] love."

No one would dispute that agape love is the divine nature of God, yet, ironically, many dispute faith as the divine nature of God. However, both love and faith are part of the divine nature of God. These are divine qualities that we can possess. We see that the apostle Peter includes faith as being part of the divine nature that we possess.

Arnold Schwarzenegger

In essence, Jesus is telling us to use the faith that God used to create the world. The faith of God made the mountains, and the faith of God can move the mountains.

For example, I may have faith in Arnold Schwarzenegger to protect me as a bodyguard. If I did, I would put my faith in him, and he would fight for me. I wouldn't have to fight. He would fight instead of me. However, if I had the muscles of Arnold, I would fight for myself.

This illustrates the difference between having faith in God and having the faith of God. Jesus is showing us that God expects us to operate in His strength and not simply be waiting on Him to do something. We can do this because we have God's muscles.

We look like God because we are born of God. To be "born of" means to be regenerated. Regeneration means to be "re-gened," to be given new genes. Genes determine our physical makeup.

In many respects I look like my physical father; I have his squinty eyes. I also look like my mother; I have her small size. The reason for this is that I have their genes. The same thing is true spiritually. Our spiritual genetic makeup is of God. We are born of God. If you could see your spirit, it would look like God. Since God is a faith-God, we are faith-children. We have His faith!

This is the lesson of the withered fig tree. Jesus took the faith of God and used it to curse a fruitless tree. He then told us to operate the same way by having the "faith of God."

How Faith Works

Jesus explained how this faith works: "Whosoever...shall believe that those things which he saith shall come to pass, he shall have whatsoever he saith" (Mark 11:23 KJV). Simply believe that what you say will come to pass, and you'll have whatever you say. Jesus is saying, "If you can believe that your words will come to pass, then you can have what you say!"

That's how God created all things. God believed that what he said would happen, and it did! God predicted the future by believing and speaking words. True faith has two components: believing and speaking. If one of these essentials is missing, then it isn't true faith.

In 2 Corinthians 4:13 we read, "It is written: 'I believed; therefore I have spoken.' With that same spirit of faith we also believe and therefore speak." Believing and speaking go together. You can't simply believe that something is going to happen and then not speak it. You must speak it!

Let's go back to the story of the fig tree in order to illustrate this truth.

> *The next day as they were leaving Beth-*
> *any, Jesus was hungry. Seeing in the*
> *distance a fig tree in leaf, he went to find*
> *out if it had any fruit. When he reached*
> *it, he found nothing but leaves, because*
> *it was not the season for figs. Then he*
> *said to the tree, "May no one ever eat*
> *fruit from you again." And his disciples*
> *heard him say it.   (Mark 11:12–14)*

Jesus spoke to the tree. He did not simply think words; He spoke words. He spoke loud enough for the disciples to hear Him.

Notice that the Bible says Jesus saw "in the distance" a fig tree. The fig tree was far away from the road which they were traveling, so Jesus got off the road and walked a long distance to see if there was fruit. The Bible only mentions Jesus walking to the tree. The disciples did not go with Jesus to the tree; they were still on the road.

This means that when Jesus spoke to the tree, He must have spoken very loudly in order for His disciples to have heard Him. He did not whisper, nor did He speak in a normal tone of voice. He shouted! By shouting to the tree, He showed that He was fully committed to believing that the tree would die.

You see, many people speak to their problems in a soft way, so that no one really knows what they believe. They speak in a way that shows that they are not truly committed to seeing the problem go.

But not Jesus. He shouted! He wanted everyone to know that this tree would be cursed. If it would not die, then they would know that Christ's faith had failed. His faith was fully committed.

Your faith must be fully committed to God's Word if you are going to see the obstacle removed. If you make any provision for failure, then success is not guaranteed.

I hear some people say, "I believe that God is going to heal me. I have rebuked the devil, so I know I'm going to be healed. But I also believe that if I die, I'm going to be with the Lord!" This sounds good, but these people are making provision for failure. Jesus did not make room for failure. He **shouted**.

This reminds me of a fellow who was waiting for a bus. A stray dog came up to him and began to lick his boots. The man nicely told the dog to leave, but the dog stayed. Repeatedly, he told the dog to leave, but the dog ignored him and continued to lick his boots. Finally, the bus arrived. The man was agitated, so with a loud command he stomped his foot and said, "I told you to go!" The dog jumped away from the man and whimpered home.

Many people act like this man. They gently say to their mountain, "Would you please go?" But the mountain refuses to listen to those whimpering words.

If you want the mountain to go, then shout with authority, "You foul mountain, I told you to go! So go!" When you speak like this, your faith starts to work.

What Do You See?

There is one more important thing I would like you to notice concerning Jesus speaking to the tree. The next morning as they passed the dead fig tree, Peter said, "Rabbi, look! The fig tree you cursed has withered!" (v. 21). Peter needed to point out to Jesus that the fig tree had died.

I read that verse one day when the Holy Spirit revealed to me the fact that Jesus was not even looking at the tree to see if its appearance was any different than the previous day. Then the Lord asked me, "Tom, if you had cursed a tree and the next day passed by that tree, would you have looked at it to see if there was a noticeable change?"

I had to humbly admit, "Yes, Lord."

Most of us would have to answer the same way. I'm sure that when the disciples were walking back down the road, the first thing they were looking for was the tree which Jesus cursed. They wanted to see if there was any change in the tree.

But Jesus was different. He did not even look to see if the tree's appearance had altered. He spoke to the tree and then went on His way, knowing that it would have to obey His faith-filled words. Jesus would not even "look" at the tree. He never went by what He saw. Jesus went "by faith, not by sight" (2 Cor. 5:7).

Faith does not look at the problem! Don't focus your eyes—your attention—on your difficulties. Don't be checking up to see if God's Word is working. Be confident that the spoken Word of faith must work; it must produce; it must predict your future.

All too often we are extremely quick to look and see if the situation has changed. If it hasn't, then we get discouraged and begin to doubt. Consequently, we don't see the obstacle removed.

I've seen people lay hands on the sick for their healing, and then immediately feel to detect any discernible difference. If they still feel the pain, then they'll declare, "I guess I'm not healed." You see, they're going by what they feel instead of by the Word of God.

You might say, "What am I supposed to say if I still feel the pain in my body?" Believe like Abraham did when God promised that his wife would have a baby. He changed his name from Abram to Abraham—before his wife got pregnant! Abraham means "father of many nations." Can you imagine being called the father of many nations while not having even one child to carry on your name?

Abraham was one "who...calls things that are not as though they were" (Rom. 4:17). We also must follow in the footsteps of his faith. He is the father of faith. He's our example!

Don't declare that the problem—the difficulty, the obstacle—is still there. Declare the end from the beginning. Predict the future of that obstacle.

Several years ago, I used to visit a nursing home. There was one ornery lady who would growl like a tiger. She was mean! It was clear that she was sick in her mind. Along with others, I would constantly pray for her deliverance by laying hands on her, but she would push our hands away from her head as we prayed for her. Obviously, she wasn't getting any better.

One warm afternoon—I'll never forget it—I sat across from her. We were separated by a long table. This time I said to the demon bothering her, loudly enough so that she and the demon could hear, "I command you, foul spirit, to come out of her."

She glared into my eyes, sulked, and said nothing! Before I walked away, I said, peering into her lifeless eyes, "Satan, this will be the last time that I will address you concerning this woman. I said that you had to leave, and you'll obey me. As far as I'm concerned, you're gone!" Then I left.

The following week as I was walking into the nursing home, the first person to catch my eye was this woman. Recognizing me, she lifted her hand high and said, "I'm free! I'm totally free!" Wow! We rejoiced in the Lord and had a wonderful time praising God. She stayed free, too.

You Are Set Free

Like Abraham, Jesus "calls things that are not as though they were." Let me show you.

On a Sabbath Jesus was teaching in one of the synagogues, and a woman was there who had been crippled by a spirit

*for eighteen years. She was bent over
and could not straighten up at all. When
Jesus saw her, he called her forward
and said to her, "Woman, you are set
free from your infirmity." Then he put
his hands on her, and immediately she
straightened up and praised God.*

(Luke 13:10–13)

Notice the sequence of events. First, Jesus called the woman forward; second, He spoke to her and said that she was set free (not that she will be set free, but that she was already set free); third, He laid His hands on her, and she straightened up and praised God.

When did Jesus say, "You are set free," after she was physically better or before she was physically better? He told her that she was set free before there was any physical appearance of healing.

Jesus was one "who...calls things that are not as though they were." He was operating in the faith of God. God "calls those things that are not as though they were." Isaiah 46:10 says that God declares the end from the beginning. God speaks the end, which is the future, from the beginning. God predicts the future. He tells us to imitate Him.

We should declare the end from the beginning. We should predict our future. We can because we have God's nature of faith. Like God and Jesus, we need to be bold in our confession.

Shout It Out

God told Zerubbabel, "What are you, O mighty mountain? Before Zerubbabel you will become level ground" (Zech. 4:7). The mountain became level ground, because the next part of the verse says, "Then he will bring out the capstone to shouts of 'God bless it! God bless it!'" The mountain was destroyed because Zerubbabel shouted to the mountain, "God bless it! God bless it!"

He shouted the blessings of God instead of simply speaking the blessings of God. He shouted the victory instead of screaming about problems. When he did, the blessings came on him and the problems left him.

During the leadership of Joshua, there was an obstacle to the promises of God. God had promised Israel the land of Canaan, but there was a big obstacle in their way—Jericho! God told Joshua to make the Israelites march around the city of Jericho for seven days and on the seventh day to march around it seven times. What were they doing? I believe that they were meditating on God's Word for victory. And when they were ready, the people gave a "loud shout" (Josh. 6:5, 20), and the walls of Jericho came tumbling down.

What did they shout? They shouted that God had given them the city! They shouted victory before they could see it. This is what God demands of you. He demands that you shout the victory before you can see any difference.

Don't shout, "Mountain, be gone!" and then say, "I don't see any change."

Don't shout, "The problem is gone!" and then say, "The problem is worse."

When you contradict yourself, you are digging up the imperishable seed of God's Word. When you speak to the mountain, you plant the seed of faith. But if you contradict your words, you dig up the seed of faith. If you dig up the seed, then there is nothing to produce the future. Your words of faith are the seeds that will predict your future.

You Can Predict Your Future
by saying...

Many are the afflictions of the righteous, but the Lord delivers me from them all.

In this world I shall have tribulations, but I am of good cheer, because Christ has overcome the world.

I am a world overcomer because I live by faith, not by sight.

I have mountain-moving faith. I speak to mountains, and they obey me.

I have Godlike faith. I believe; therefore, I speak. I have the spirit of faith. This faith overcomes obstacles.

I put on God's fighting clothes. I put on the belt of truth. I have my feet covered with the preparation of the gospel of peace. I have my breastplate of righteousness in place. I put on the helmet of salvation and take up the sword of the Spirit, which is the Word of God. And above all else, I use the shield of faith to guard me from the arrows of the evil one.

I am shielded by God's faith and power.

I am a participant in the divine nature. I have God's faith, God's peace, God's joy, God's love, God's patience, and God's strength.

I am regenerated. I have God's spiritual genes. If you've seen me, you've seen the Father. As Christ is, so am I in this world.

Chapter 14

Growing Up Spiritually

The Bible likens spiritual growth to physical growth: "Like newborn babies, crave pure spiritual milk, so that by it you may grow up in your salvation" (1 Pet. 2:2). When you were first born again, your spirit was a baby spirit. It was complete but not matured. In the natural, a baby is complete—it has hands, legs, eyes, and muscles. Even though he has legs, he cannot walk because the legs have not been developed enough to walk. In time, though, he will walk.

The same is true of our faith. We can speak faith-words as a baby Christian and get some results. But as we grow, our words will become more powerful because our faith has grown. At the same time, we grow in wisdom and in the ability to hear God's voice so that we don't just blab words without the anointing of the Holy Spirit. As we mature in the Lord, we learn to speak what we hear God saying; therefore, we will receive nearly everything we confess.

I believe that ten years from now my words will be even more powerful than they are today. I believe that the time between my confession of faith and the time I receive will get shorter and shorter. My words are working faster and faster as I grow in faith. This should happen to you as well.

There was a man in the Bible whose words always came to pass. His name was Samuel. The Bible says, "The LORD was with Samuel as he grew up, and he let none of his words fall to the ground" (1 Sam. 3:19). Everything that Samuel said happened. The reason is because Samuel "grew up." He learned to wait upon the Lord for the revelation of God's will. When he received that revelation, he also meditated on that word from God until he was ready to speak the word of God.

This is what God wants us to do. He desires for us to "grow up" by waiting for Him until we receive the revelation of His will. Once we do, we should meditate on that revelation until it becomes absolutely real to us. And when that happens we are ready to speak forth the Word of God.

When you do, God will not let any of your words fall to the ground, too. The Word of God spoken out of you mouth will predict your future.

You Can Predict Your Future
by saying...

I am growing up in my salvation.

My faith is growing exceedingly fast.

I am learning to listen to God's voice and obey His Word.

I refuse to say anything that I don't hear my Father saying. I speak only what I hear my Father speak.

God has a wonderful plan for me. He plans to prosper me and not to harm me. He plans to give me hope and a future.

I trust God. I do not fear the future, because God is in control of my life.

About the Author

Tom Brown is the founder and pastor of two growing congregations in El Paso, Texas, Word of Life Church and River of Life Church. Among his duties as pastor, he finds time to publish his city's largest and longest running Christian publication called *Good News, El Paso*. He is also president of the Charismatic Bible School which is equipping believers for full-time ministry. He is known for being an outstanding preacher of the Gospel as well as one who moves mightily in the gifts of the Spirit. He lives in El Paso with his wife, Sonia, and three children—Justin, Faith, and Caleb.